Author
Author Andrew Coe was born into a family of Mexico scholars and visited all the major archeological sites as a child. Based in New York, he has traveled the world extensively and now works as a freelance author specializing in Latin America. His books include two other Odyssey Guides, to Mexico and Cuba.

Photographer
Based in Mexico, photographer Kal Muller has experienced, photographed and written about many of the most interesting and isolated places of the world. He has produced a number of books and his photographs and articles have appeared in *National Geographic*, *Geo* and many other prestigious magazines.

(previous page) Iglesia de la Virgen de Guadalupe

MEXICO CITY

Andrew Coe
Photography by Kal Muller

© 1999, 1995, 1994 Odyssey Publications Ltd
Maps © 1999, 1995, 1994 Odyssey Publications Ltd

Odyssey Publications Ltd, 1004 Kowloon Centre, 29–43 Ashley Road,
Tsim Sha Tsui, Kowloon, Hong Kong
Tel. (852) 2856 3896; Fax. (852) 2565 8004; E-mail: odyssey@asiaonline.net

Distribution in the United Kingdom, Ireland and Europe by
Hi Marketing Ltd, 38 Carver Road, London, SE24 9LT, UK

Distribution in the United States of America by
W.W. Norton & Company, Inc., New York

Library of Congress Catalog Card Number has been requested.

ISBN: 962-217-581-3

Grateful acknowledgment is made to the following authors and publishers:

W. W. Norton & Co Inc for *Five Letters 1519–1526* by Hernando Cortés, translated by J Bayard Morris
© W. W. Norton & Co Inc; Viking Penguin, a division of Penguin Books USA Inc for
'In Memory of Tlatelolco' from *Massacre in Mexico* by Elena Poniatowska © 1971 by Ediciones Era.
English translation © 1975 The Viking Press; Penguin (UK) and Viking Penguin (US) for
On the Road by Jack Kerouac © 1955 Jack Kerouac; Alfred A Knopf Inc and Random House UK for
My Last Sigh by Luis Buñuel. Translation © 1983 by Alfred A Knopf Inc; University of Oklahoma Press
for *Book of the Gods and Rights and the Ancient Calendar* by Fray Diego Durán © 1971 University of
Oklahoma Press

Editor: David Clive Price
Series Editor: Jane Finden-Crofts
Illustrations Editor: John Oliver
Design: Aubrey Tse and Teresa Ho
Maps: Bai Yiliang and Au Yeung Chui Kwai
Cover Concept: Margaret Lee

Front and back cover photography: Robert & Linda Mitchell
Photography by Kal Muller
Additional illustrations courtesy of Hermanos Mayo, Archivo General de la Nación 11, 38, 146;
Enrique Díaz, Archivo General de la Nación 84, 109, 119, 183, 185; Agustín Casasola, Fototeca del
INAH 22, 23, 26, 42, 59, 87, 153, 192; Andrew Coe 123, 126, 129

Production by Twin Age Ltd, Hong Kong
Printed in China

The National Museum of Art

Contents

Introduction

Mexico City has been the capital of Latin America for over half a millennium. In the time of the Aztecs it was one of the wonders of the world, a shining, white city that housed the hub of a great empire. Armies of warriors and traders advanced from here to conquer foreign lands and returned with vast riches of gold jewelry, jade sculptures, rare animals, robes made of feathers and on and on. After the Spanish Conquest, Mexico City became the seat of the colonial government that ruled New Spain from California to Guatemala. Mountains of silver ore were found in the provinces and wealth poured into the capital. European visitors were dazzled by the opulence of the creole aristocracy; the capital's poets, playwrights and scientists were lauded by Old World intellectuals. From the mix of Spanish and Indian, a new and distinctive Mexican culture was born. European baroque architecture was transformed into the churrigueresque, a home-grown rococo style that transported the viewer with its lushness and depth. In the 19th century, the capital was a city of churrigueresque and neo-classical church towers. Visitors agreed that, in the clear air and framed against the snow-capped volcanoes, Mexico City was one of the most beautiful places in the world. In this century, the capital has boomed, leaving behind the colonial city. Factories were built, streets were widened and vast new suburbs spread across the dry lake beds. Although Mexico City lost much of its charm, a new and vigorous urban culture percolated out of the slums. Films, paintings, literature, dances and music were created that captured not only the local audience but Spanish-speakers around the world. Diego Rivera and other famous muralists led what was called the 'Mexican Renaissance'; the comic Cantinflas became an international star; and readers celebrated the poetry of Octavio Paz and the fiction of Carlos Fuentes. Today, the most popular program on Russian television is a Mexican soap opera.

Chac mool, Anthropology Museum

Unfortunately, Mexico City's severe problems tend to conceal its glories from visitors. There are simply too many people, cars and factories in the Valley of Mexico, producing too much pollution and using its dwindling resources too fast. Nevertheless, a little touristic adventurousness will be repaid in full. Beneath the grime Mexico City has incredible cultural riches that most visitors barely tap. Start at the Zócalo, one of the great plazas of the world and the focal point of the Mexican nation. Two of the country's most powerful institutions—the Presidency and the Catholic Church, symbolized by the magnificent National Cathedral—line the plaza. A few steps to the north is the ancient center of the Aztec universe, the Templo Mayor ('Great Temple'), which housed the statues of the gods Tláloc and Huitzilopochtli, the main Aztec deities.

The Wrestler, *Olmec Culture, Anthropology Museum*

The Zócalo and the surrounding blocks make up the Centro Historico, a zone of fine old colonial palaces and churches, many built on Aztec foundations.

Next, head west to Chapultepec Park and the Anthropology Museum, one of the greatest collections in the world, to put the Aztec world into perspective. Here are the finest objects yet discovered from the great pre-Hispanic civilizations, of which the Aztecs were the last. With this introduction to Mexico, you can now let your fancy be your guide. You can see colonial Mexico in the history museum in Chapultepec Castle, in the fine churches and museums around the Zócalo and the Alameda Park, and in the beautiful neighborhoods of San Angel and Coyoacán to the south.

The achievements of modern Mexico may be seen in the incredible murals sprinkled all over the city, in Chapultepec Park's modern art gallery and the Carrillo Gil museum in San Angel and in the sprawling University City. For entertainment the choices are endless: bullfights, *lucha libre* (professional wrestling), boxing, movies, theater, nightclubs, concerts, burlesque shows, dance halls and, best of all, the joyous anarchy of the Plaza Garibaldi at night. Mexico City has been a shopper's paradise since the Aztec era; their legacy lives on in the vast markets at La Merced. There are dozens of excellent crafts stores here; the Zona Rosa is a glitzy, Americanized shopping mecca, and the outskirts are home to huge malls like Perisur and Plaza Satélite. And do not forget to eat! Despite its reputation, most of Mexico City's better restaurants are safe and the dishes they produce are the finest Mexican food in the world.

History

History weighs heavily in Mexico, in a way that is reminiscent of the former Soviet Union. Ancient schisms, like that between the European and New World cultures, have yet to be fully bridged. Passionate debates are still held about historical figures, including Columbus and Cortés, dead almost 500 years. The spirits of long-dead Mexican politicians are resurrected by every presidential regime to serve as its ideological icons; Benito Juárez and Francisco Madero are two of the most popular. One reason for this practice may be that the government, ruled by the same party since the 1920s, undergoes occasional crises of legitimacy and thus needs to wrap itself in the glory of past patriots. The most recent, and surprising, resurrection is that of the dictator Porfirio Díaz, who for eight decades had been cast into political oblivion. President Salinas's government has just refurbished his image, perhaps because it desperately wants foreign investment, one of the centerpieces of the Díaz regime.

One historical fact that a Mexican politician might prefer to ignore is that Mexico City was not always the most important place in Mesoamerica. In fact, it did not even exist until the 14th century. Millions of years ago, a volcanic eruption blocked the Valley of Mexico's streams from flowing to the sea; the valley became what is technically known as a closed hydrographic system, or a basin, and wide, shallow salt- and freshwater lakes formed at the bottom. The valley's ecology before the arrival of the Spanish has been described by researchers in Eden-like terms. The climate was mild and moist year round; the hills were covered with dense forests; and both the lakes and the land abounded in wildlife. During the Pleistocene era, herds of now extinct mammals gathered around the lush lakeshore and attracted the arrows and knives of early hunters. Many lively ceramic figurines and utensils have been found in Formative-era (1200 BC–AD 150) tombs from the lakeside settlements at Tlatilco, Zacatenco and Cuicuilco. The most important of these sites is Cuicuilco, just south of UNAM, which was buried under a lava flow from the Xictli volcano around AD 100. The highlight here is a circular step pyramid that was topped with altars and incense burners dedicated to the Fire God. During the Early Classic era, the great city of Teotihuacán rose in the northeastern corner of the valley to become the dominant force in Mesoamerica. When factional conflicts and droughts led to the collapse of the Toltec empire and the abandonment of Tula in the 12th century, the Toltecs moved into the Valley of Mexico and settled on the hill of Chapultepec and in Culhuacán (now south-central Mexico City). They were followed by other migrating tribes, like the Chichimeca, Acolhua, Otomi and Tepanecs, who divided the land around the lake into city-states. These intermarried with the Toltecs, and each gradually began to profess that they were the true heirs of that fallen empire.

Around AD 1300 a ragged group of wanderers entered the valley carrying an image of their blood-thirsty god Huitzilopochtli, the God of the Sun and of War. Better known as the Aztecs, they called them-selves the Mexica and had departed their now-mythical island home of Aztlan about AD 1111 on the orders of Huitzilopochtli. Speaking through his priests, the God had foreseen that they would conquer 'all peoples of the universe'. The other residents of the valley considered them savages and evicted them from their first home at Chapultepec.

The Coyolxauhqui stone shortly after discovery

The Culhuas hired them as mercenaries and gave them a snake-infested strip of volcanic rock as their home. The Aztecs surprised the Culhuas by thriving; they ate all the snakes, were brutally efficient as mercenaries and began to intermarry with the local aristocratic lineages. One day Huitzilopochtli decreed that a noble virgin be sacrificed to become his godly consort. The Aztecs asked a Culhua ruler to give them one of his daughters to be their sovereign, took her back to their settlement, then sacrificed her and invited the ruler to a feast at which an Aztec priest danced in her flayed skin.

The Culhuas, appalled and frightened by the Aztecs' crime, took up arms and drove them from their settlement into the marshes of the lake. As the Aztecs shivered through a long night among the reeds, Huitzilopochtli spoke again and told them that they would find a new home nearby, on an island where an eagle seated on a nopal cactus was eating a serpent. This eagle is now the symbol of Mexico and is enshrined on the national flag. The Aztecs named their settlement Tenochtitlán

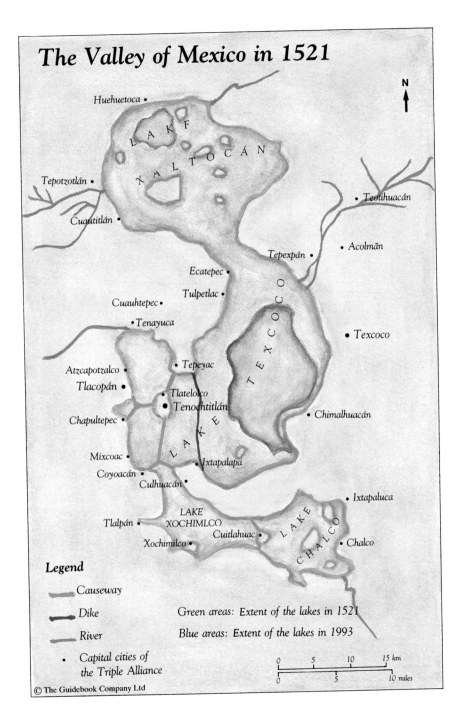

The Valley of Mexico in 1521

N

Huehuetoca •

L A K E

X A L T O C Á N

Tepotzotlán •

• Teotihuacán

Cuautitlán •

• Acolmän

Tepexpán •

Ecatepec •

Tulpetlac •

Cuauhtepec •

• Tenayuca

• Texcoco

L
A
K
E

T
E
X
C
O
C
O

• Tepeyac

Atzcapotzalco •

Tlacopán •

• Tlatelolco

• Tenochtitlán

Chapultepec •

• Chimalhuacán

L
A
K
E

Mixcoac •

• Ixtapalapa

Coyoacán •

Culhuacán •

• Ixtapaluca

LAKE
XOCHIMLCO

L
A
K
E

Tlalpán •

Cuitlahuac •

Xochimilco •

C
H
A
L
C
O

• Chalco

Legend

——— Causeway

——— Dike

——— River

• Capital cities of
the Triple Alliance

Green areas: Extent of the lakes in 1521

Blue areas: Extent of the lakes in 1993

0   5   10   15 km

0   5   10 miles

© The Guidebook Company Ltd

('Place of the Cactus') and began to prosper by growing food on *chinampas*, artificially constructed platforms, and by hunting and fishing on the rich network of lakes. Tenochtitlán's location proved crucial to its subsequent growth, because far more goods could be transported by canoe than via the only land-based beast of burden, the human back. When the town became too crowded, a group of traders settled on an island to the north they named Tlatelolco. Those that remained in Tenochtitlán, who called themselves the Mexica (from which the name 'Mexico' derives), were dominated by warriors; they hired themselves out as mercenaries to the Tepanecs, who were trying to conquer the valley. The Tepanec ruler, Tezozómoc, was a ruthless Machiavellian who delighted in playing factions off each other and taught the Aztecs many lessons in imperial politics. Tezozómoc's successor, his inept and unpopular son Maxlatzin, hated the Aztecs and was afraid of their newfound status. He decided to destroy them, but the Aztec king, Itzcoatl, and his minister of state, Tlacaelel, resolved to fight rather than flee. They convinced the Texcocans, Tlaxcalans and Huexotzingans to form an alliance, besieging, then capturing Azcapotzalco, the Tepanec capital. Thereafter the valley was ruled by a triple alliance of the Aztecs, the Texcocans and the Tacubans. The Aztecs quickly emerged as the dominant partner and captured the remaining towns around the lake, including Coyoacán and Xochi-milco. Tlacaelel became the power behind the Aztec throne and forged the new political and economic structure of the empire. He rewrote Aztec history to trace Aztec lineage directly back to the glorious Toltecs and encouraged Aztec expansion by emphasizing that Huitzilopochtli needed the hearts of enemies to win his daily battle with Night.

Between 1440 and 1468, Tlacaelel's brother, Motecuhzoma I reigned, and his armies expanded the realm as far as Oaxaca and the Huasteca of northern Veracruz. During this period the first Flowery Wars were fought; these were arranged battles with the nearby but never conquered states of Chalco, Huexotzingo and Tlaxcala, whose sole purpose was to provide captives for ritual sacrifice. In 1487, the militaristic Aztec king, Ahuitzotl, celebrated the completion of the Great Temple (Templo Mayor) with the sacrifice of as many as 20,000 captives in a five-day festival. Ahuitzotl was succeeded in 1502 by a very different type of ruler, the philosopher-king Motecuhzoma II. ('Motecuhzoma' is the Nahuatl name for the Spanish 'Moctezuma' and the English 'Montezuma'). Although he continued the Aztec expansion, Motecuhzoma II emphasized the consolidation of lands already conquered into the vast system of tribute flowing into Tenochtitlán. By this time the Aztec capital was a wonder of the New World, with a population of over 200,000 and a vast network of canals filled with canoes and lined with whitewashed stone palaces, all heading toward the magnificent hub of the Great Temple. Tlatelolco to the north held the great markets that were the largest in Mesoamerica. Motecuhzoma's fatal flaw was that he was deeply superstitious and had a corps of magicians and soothsayers working for him.

He was especially fearful of bad omens, and they started coming fast and furious—a comet, a mysterious fire in the Great Temple and, in 1518, news of a mountain that moved on the water and was populated by white-skinned and bearded men (probably Juan de Grijalva's expedition).

When Cortés appeared off the Tabasco coast in 1519, Motecuhzoma had spies waiting on the shore, who sent detailed reports to the capital. He feared that the Spaniard was the legendary Toltec ruler, Quetzalcoatl, returning from the east to herald the downfall of the Aztec empire. By the time he realized that the Spaniards were mere mortals, the conquistadors had penetrated deep into Aztec territory. Cortés' arrival in the Valley of Mexico caused great alarm among the Aztec population, 'as if they had eaten hallucinating mushrooms, or seen some dreadful vision'. Motecuhzoma met the Spanish with expressions of welcome and quartered them in a palace while secretly planning to kill them.

However, it was Cortés who made the first move; hearing that six of his soldiers had been killed by Aztec troops in Veracruz, he took Motecuhzoma hostage. Militant members of the Aztec nobility stood outside waiting to slaughter the Spanish while their ruler vacillated about giving the order to attack. His delay seemed justified when a punitive expedition from Cuba led by Pánfilo Narváez landed in Veracruz to arrest Cortés. Cortés left Motecuhzoma in the custody of 80 soldiers under Pedro de Alvarado and quick-marched to the coast. Before he left, he rashly smashed the most important Aztec idols, further antagonizing the Indians. The Narváez expedition proved a boon to Cortés, because after his troops defeated them, many of the gold-hungry soldiers joined his forces. Meanwhile, Alvarado led his men into an Aztec festival and, fearing it presaged an uprising, systematically slaughtered dozens of priests. When Cortés returned, the Aztecs cut off all food and water to the Spanish troops and replaced Motecuhzoma with his more militant brother, Cuitláhuac. Fighting began, and the conquistadors forced Motecuhzoma onto a battlement to plead with his people to lay down their arms. He was answered by a shower of stones that killed him. Cortés decided that it was time to flee and told his troops that they could take whatever gold and jewels their arms could carry. On 10 July 1520, known as the *Noche Triste* ('Sad Night'), the Spanish escaped along a causeway; the Aztecs discovered their flight and destroyed the bridges, forcing the Spanish to swim. With the enemy at their heels and weighed down with booty, most of the conquistadors drowned in the canals, and only Cortés and a fraction of his men survived. The Aztecs lost the chance to complete their victory by neglecting to hunt down and kill the fleeing Spaniards.

For almost a year, the conquistadors rested on the coast, welcomed reinforcements drawn by news of gold and conquered the city-states in the area that still paid tribute to the Aztecs. The populations that resisted were enslaved and marked with a brand on their faces. The Aztecs knew that war was coming, but they were weakened by a smallpox epidemic that killed Cuitláhuac. On 1 June 1521 backed by Tlaxcalan troops, the Spaniards attacked the vastly larger Aztec force along the three major causeways and with war brigantines on the water. The Aztecs won the first battles but wasted time and energy in capturing the enemy alive (for sacrificial purposes) rather than killing them immediately. Cortés himself was about to be sacrificed when his troops saved him. The Spaniards changed tactics and cut off the food and water supplies to Tenochtitlán. Then they slowly tightened the circle around the capital, destroying the Aztec buildings as they advanced. The Aztecs finally realized that defeat was inevitable, and their last ruler, Cuauhtemoc, was captured as he tried to escape. During the days that followed, Tenochtitlán was abandoned and then sacked and burned by the Spanish and their Tlaxcalan allies, who also celebrated with human sacrifices when the Spanish were out of the way. The fleeing Aztecs spread smallpox and other European diseases to the rest of Mexico, beginning the next cycle of conquest.

Cortés established the first Spanish government in the more pleasant city of Coyoacán to the south. In 1522, he ordered the razing of the Aztec palaces and temples around the Great Plaza and began to rebuild Tenochtitlán, renamed 'Mexico', as the capital of New Spain. His architects kept the quadrangular Aztec plan and, perhaps unwittingly, designed the first true Renaissance city, with broad avenues and plazas and no confining city walls. The Spanish lived in the center around the Great Plaza and the Indian neighborhoods lay in the outskirts on the other side of a canal. This division of races was considered crucial to Spanish plans for the evangelization and colonization of the natives. The first new buildings were fort-like palaces and churches built on the Aztec foundations and from Aztec stones, including the Palacio Real, the Palacio de Cortés (now the Palacio Nacional) and the Cathedral. With the Aztec treasures gone forever at the bottom of the lake, the conquistadors now hoped to gain wealth through plantations, mining and Indian slave labor. Little did they know that Charles V of Spain had other ideas.

The Spanish empire was one of the most centralized in Europe; the Crown was as jealous of potential internal rivals as it was hostile to external threats. When Charles V saw that a group of greedy and independent soldiers had miraculously conquered a huge and wealthy land and were planning on becoming its ruling class, he immediately moved to seize control. Lawyer-bureaucrats, called *letrados*, were sent from Spain to whittle down the conquistadors' land and power, starting with Cortés himself. This became the leitmotif of the colonial era: every time New Spain became wealthier, the Crown, bogged down in endless European wars, would devise new means of ensuring that the money went directly into its coffers. Mexico's élite naturally resented the powers of the *letrados*, who quickly became fantastically corrupt

The Final Battle

As soon as day broke I assembled all my men, having previously ordered Albarado to wait for me in the market-place and not to attack until I arrived, and when we were all together and the brigs had taken up their position on the further side of the houses which the enemy still occupied, I gave orders to my men that on the sound of a musket shot they should attack the small portion which remained and force the enemy to throw themselves into the water at the very place where the brigs were; I warned them to keep a sharp look-out for Guatimucin [Cuautémoc] and to make every effort to take him alive, for that done all fighting would cease. I myself went up to one of the roof-tops and before the combat spoke with several of the enemy chiefs whom I knew asking them why their lord was unwilling to come to me in person; for since they were in such straits they would do well to avoid acting in such a way that all must perish, and should bid him come forward without fear; upon this two of the chiefs seemed to depart and speak with him. In a short time one of the most important of all the chieftains returned with them, by name Ciguacoacin, the captain and governor of them all, whose advice was taken in all things pertaining to the war. I greeted him kindly to reassure him, and finally he told me that their ruler was utterly detemined not to come to me and would rather die in the city, the which grieved me much. Seeing therefore his determination I bade him return to his men and bid them prepare themselves for battle for I intended to attack them and kill them all: and on this he departed. More than five hours were thus spent in these bargainings. Those left in the city stood and walked on piles of dead bodies, others were already in the water either attempting to swim or drowning in the great lake where their canoes were; such in a word was the affliction which they were in that it was beyond the wit of man to understand how they could endure it: all the time an infinite number of men, women and children were making their way towards us: and in order that they might escape the quicker many were jostled into the water and drowned amidst that vast multitude of corpses; for as it afterwards appeared, the drinking of salt water, hunger and the stench of dead bodies had worked such havoc upon them that in all more than fifty thousand souls had thus perished. And in order that we should not realize their plight these bodies were neither thrown into the water where our brigs would have come across them nor taken out of doors and exposed in the streets where we should have been able to see them. I myself visited some of the streets which remained to them and found the dead heaped one upon the other, so that one was forced to walk upon them. As the inhabitants of the city were now coming out of their own accord towards us, I provided that there should be Spaniards posted in every street to prevent our allies from killing the wretches who thus abandoned their city, and who were too numerous to count. I likewise warned the leaders of our allies that none of these people was to be killed; yet the numbers were such that it was impossible to prevent them and some fifteen thousand must have lost their lives that day: yet the chieftains and warriors still remained in certain corners, rooftops and boats, where no kind of dissimulation could longer profit them, since their ruin and helplessness were only too plain. Seeing that night was drawing on and that they still refused to surrender I trained two guns on them to see if that would move them, for to have permitted our allies to attack them would have caused greater suffering than the guns, which in effect did them some damage. But this profiting nothing, I ordered the musket to be fired and almost immediately the corner which they held was rushed and taken and those that remained were thrown into the water: others surrendered without striking a blow; the brigs immediately entered the inner lake and broke right into

when they saw the potential of this virgin territory. The *letrados* were followed by merchants, adventurers and, in 1524, by the first Catholic missionaries. Following their goal of converting the Indians, the missionaries helped to push the boundaries of New Spain from Guatemala to California. Their holy work was heralded by European diseases like smallpox, measles and typhus, which decimated the Indian population. Anthropologists believe that before the arrival of the Spanish, the Valley of Mexico was home to 1.5 million Indians; 50 years later they numbered just 70,000. Those that survived were put to work building the Spanish city and working on the plantations that surrounded it.

For the 200 years following the Conquest, there were relatively few major upheavals in Mexico City. Perhaps the most important change was that the original colonial society of a tiny Spanish ruling class imposed on a mass of Indians was gradually being replaced by one that was distinctly 'Mexican' as we know it today. That is not to say that alterations were not taking place. In fact, Motecuhzoma would not have recognized the valley of Mexico in 1721. The thick forests were gone, chopped down for charcoal and construction materials and to act as pilings for the colonial buildings sinking into the soft soil. The Spanish preferred the hills bare, because it reminded them of home. After a flood that covered Mexico City for five long years between 1629 and 1634, a 100-year project of draining the network of lakes began. Both these changes to the valley's ecology have had drastic consequences that continue to this day. In the center of the city, the blocks around the Zócalo may have had a new shine put on them by the infusion of capital from provincial silver mines—European visitors marvelled at the palaces and churches, many in the elaborate, home-grown, churrigueresque style, and at the ostentation of the jewel-encrusted élite promenading in the Alameda—but beneath the finery was a city of poverty and violence. A new urban underclass sprang up, personified by the *lépero*, a vagabond used to living by his wits and with a marked tendency to crime. Since society was regulated by an elaborate caste system based on race, determining every aspect of life, all chances for betterment of one's lot were closed off. Popular unrest led to spontaneous outbursts of mob violence, like the Tumult of 1692, in which the Palacio Real and other government buildings were torched, but the question of race still remained unresolved. In 1790, when workmen discovered the Aztec Calendar Stone and the Coatlicue statue (both now in the Anthropology Museum) just east of the Cathedral, the Catholic Church immediately buried them in a convent courtyard as pagan idols, unfit for Christian eyes. However, a scholarly priest named Fray Servando campaigned to have them displayed in order to improve academic knowledge of the Aztecs. So began the long fight to convince creole opinion that Indians were not just beasts of burden but human beings who had something to teach Mexican society.

By the beginning of the 19th century, Mexico City symbolized everything that was wrong with New Spain. Here was the seat of the Royalist government that assessed huge taxes, promulgated laws that crushed economic enterprise (even making wine was forbidden) and was also monstrously corrupt. For the next century the city was the target of provincial armies' rage and of the imperial designs of foreign invaders. After Independence in 1821, all emblems of Spanish power were erased from city buildings and the equestrian statue of Charles IV was removed from the Great Plaza, now called the Zócalo. The decades that followed were marked by political and economic chaos that led to great destitution; thousands joined the ranks of the *léperos* on the city streets. In 1847, an invading American army led by General Winfield Scott arrived at the outskirts of the capital. After victories at Contreras and Churubusco to the south, Scott's troops defeated the Mexicans at Molino del Rey in a bloody battle during which 2,000 Mexicans and 700 Americans died. Scott advanced to the last Mexican position, the castle on Chapultepec Hill, and stormed it on

September 13th. The last defenders were young military cadets, six of whom threw themselves from the ramparts rather than surrender. They are enshrined in the Mexican national pantheon as the Child Heroes (*Niños Héroes*) of Chapultepec. In the 1850s, the reins of power were seized by Benito Juárez, a stern Zapotec Indian who was determined to do away with the greed and corruption found in the capital. A centerpiece of his reforms was a bill greatly reducing the power and privilege of the Catholic Church, Mexico's largest landowner. Many of Mexico City's churches and convents were converted into offices, hotels and private homes. The French army ousted Juárez and replaced him with the ineffectual Emperor Maximilian, who had a great love for the trappings of royalty and expected his capital to reflect that. He rebuilt Chapultepec Castle as a palatial home and constructed the Paseo de la Reforma (originally named the Avenue of the Empire) to take his carriage to the Palacio Real. Stability finally returned to Mexico under the repressive regime of Porfirio Díaz. He wanted Mexico City to become a modern, European-style capital

The Zócalo, flanked by the Cathedral and the National Palace

The revolutionary leaders Francisco Villa (seated second from left) and Emiliano Zapata (fourth from left) meet over dinner at the Palacio Nacional, Agustín Casasola

and inaugurated a host of public works projects that changed the face of the city. Electric lights arrived in 1880, mule-drawn omnibuses were replaced by electric trollies and the first planned *colonias* ('neighborhoods') were built along Reforma. By the time of the 1910 Centennial of Independence gala, Mexico City shone with a French-style Porfiriato gloss, exemplified by the white marble monument to Juárez at the south side of the Alameda. However, a huge gulf had opened between the capital's Europeanized élite and the provincial poor and middle class. Less than a year later, revolution broke out and Díaz was forced into exile.

Between 1910 and 1920, the revolutionary armies of Zapata, Villa and Carranza inflicted a decade of violence and starvation on the city. Their initial enemy was General Victoriano Huerta, who had masterminded the assassination of the democratically elected liberal, Francisco I Madero. As Huerta's capital, Mexico City bore the brunt of the revolutionaries' rage. Huerta was forced into exile in 1914, and thereafter the revolutionaries fought against each other to decide who would be able to lead the triumphant march to the Presidential Palace. Meanwhile, Mexico City's residents, whom the revolutionaries suspected still held Huertista sympathies, slowly starved. In time, however, the city regained its strength since it was not as badly ravaged as the countryside.

After the Revolution the new political leaders began transforming the capital into a modern city. The first art-deco skyscrapers were built, and new factories began to dot the surrounding fields. Mexico City became the land of opportunity and millions of the provincial poor and middle class flocked here. A new urban sensibility was born: songs, movies, comic books and theater reflected the perils and joys of immigration; the slums and the *demi-monde* of dance halls, bordellos and cantinas were glorified in popular culture. Slum characters, like that of the comic Cantinflas, became celebrities; *cantinflismo*, the art of spouting streams of verbiage without saying anything, entered Spanish dictionaries. Mexico City suddenly found itself at the forefront of artistic revolution when a group of muralists, including Diego Rivera, José Clemente Orozco and David Siquieros, attracted worldwide attention for covering the walls of government buildings with bold political statements. In the 1930s and 1940s, this cultural ferment was fostered by the arrival of Republicans fleeing Franco in Spain, and then by Europeans escaping from Nazism. World War II, bringing with it massive defense contracts from the Allies, was a boom time for Mexico. The capital's population explosion continued apace.

Between 1952 and 1964, the Regent (mayor) of Mexico City was a man named Ernesto Uruchurtu who was determined to erase the antiquated and 'unhygienic' city, replacing it with one that was modern and dynamic. Old neighborhoods were destroyed to make way for highways to the suburbs, including the Periférico, Insurgentes Sur and the northern extension of Reforma. Huge public works projects, like University City, the Ciudad Tlatelolco housing project and the Anthropology Museum, were meant not only to transform the city but also to alter radically the way Mexicans lived—all culminating in the 1968 Olympics. However, the year before the Olympics was marked by the ever-growing demonstrations of left-wing students, who were confronted by increasingly violent police and soldiers. The conservative President Díaz Ordaz decided to squash the protest before they embarrassed him in front of a world audience. On 2 October 1968, he ordered soldiers to open fire on a night meeting in Tlatelolco's plaza; hundreds of students and bystanders were systematically massacred. This tragedy and the political repression that followed has left scars on the national psyche that have yet to heal.

Zapatista revolutionaries sipping chocolate, Agustín Casasola

Massacre

On the night of 2 October 1968, just before the Olympic Games, government soldiers fired on a crowd of student demonstrators in the Plaza de las Tres Culturas, Tlatelolco, Mexico City.

Darkness breeds violence
and violence seeks darkness
to carry out its bloody deeds.
That is why on October 2 they waited for nightfall
so that no one could see the hand
that held the gun, only its sudden lightning flash.

And who is there in the last pale light of day?
Who is the killer?
Who are those who writhe in agony, those who are dying?
Those who flee in panic, leaving their shoes behind?
Those who fall into the dark pit of prison?
Those rotting in a hospital?
Those who become forever mute, from sheer terror?

Who are they? How many are there? Not a one.
Not a trace of any of them the next day.
By dawn the following morning the Plaza had been swept clean.
The lead stories in the papers
were about the weather.
And on TV, on the radio, at the movie theaters
the programs went on as scheduled,
no interruptions for an announcement,
not a moment of reverent silence at the festivities.
(Because the celebration went right on, according to plan.)

Don't search for something there are no signs of now:
traces of blood, dead bodies,
because it was all an offering to a goddess,
the Eater of Excrement.
Don't search in the files, because no records have been kept.

But I feel pain when I probe right here: here in my memory
it hurts, so the wound is real. Blood mingling with blood
and if I call it my own blood, I betray one and all.

I remember, we remember.
This is our way of hastening the dawn,
of shedding a ray of light on so many consciences
that bear a heavy burden,
on angry pronouncements, yawning prison gates,
faces hidden behind masks.
I remember, let us all remember
until justice comes to sit among us.

Rosario Castellanos, 'In Memory of Tlatelolco',
from Elena Poniatowska, Massacre in Mexico,
trans Helen R Lane, 1975

Selling 'Judases' to be burned on the Saturday before Easter Sunday, Agustin Casasola

In the 1970s, planners began to realize that the city's expansion was out of control. The first Metro line opened in 1969 (and now covers most of the city) but it hardly put a dent in the burgeoning growth of vehicular traffic. A new phenomenon—smog—began to blanket the ground every morning and cause serious health problems for children and old people. New immigrants, desperate from rural poverty, were forced to settle in vast slums like Netzahualcoyotl that spread across the dry, salt-poisoned bed of Lake Texcoco. Today, experts estimate that the total population for the Federal District and the adjacent metropolitan areas in the State of Mexico is over 20 million. The pressure on the water supply is so great that the water table has dropped, causing the city to sink and many old buildings, including the Cathedral, to lean to one side. As if that were not enough, at 7.19 am on 19 September 1985, an earthquake measuring 8.1 on the Richter Scale killed tens of thousands, left many more homeless and destroyed dozens of poorly built modern buildings in the downtown area. The government's slow response so enraged residents that they decided the moment had come to finally turn their city around. Citizens' groups calling for political and ecological change almost toppled the government in 1988, and they have continued to put pressure on both local and national administrations. Under first President Salinas and now Zedillo, the federal government has taken drastic steps to heal the city's ravaged environment. Unfortunately, however, levels of major pollutants continue to climb. In 1995 the devaluation of the peso caused a noticeable increase in urban crime (much of it committed by ex-policemen fired in an ongoing anti-corruption drive). The middle and upper classes have begun leaving the capital for healthier lives in the provinces, while millions of urban poor are left to fight for the very basics of a decent life. One ray of hope was the 1997 election of Cuauhtemoc Cárdenas as the city's first non-PRI mayor since the Revolution. He has promised to clean out the old corrupt institutions and institute a new, egalitarian urban policy. Although Mexico City's problems seem intractable, he has made a promising start.

Geography

The cornucopia-shaped landmass of Mexico is belted east-west across the middle by a range of mountains called the Volcanic Cordillera. This is a region of snow-capped volcanoes, lakes and fertile valleys. In the center of this region, the largest and most important valley is the Valley of Mexico (2,100 meters, 7,000 feet above sea level), ringed on three sides by a line of volcanoes. The Valley of Mexico is unique in that it has no outlet; it is a basin (or was until the construction of a huge drainage canal and tunnel in the 17th century). The emergence of those volcanoes millions of years ago sent a lava flow across the valley's natural southern outlet, with the result that rainwater and springs flowed to the center of the basin where there lay a network of shallow lakes, now almost totally dry. Although there has been no significant volcanic eruption since the explosion of the Xictli volcano around AD 100, the area remains seismically active. The last two major earthquakes in Mexico City occurred in 1957 and 1985. The Valley of Mexico's position in the center of the country and unique geological structure played crucial roles in its emergence as the hub of Latin America. The ring of mountains protected it from foreign invaders, yet a system of roads allowed the valley's armies to lead attacks in all four directions on lower-lying neighbors. One of the reasons Tenochtitlán grew to such magnificence is that its main roads were canals; they could carry much more on boats than on their chief beast of burden, the human back. In this century, the valley's strong points have proved detrimental to its citizens. The ring of mountains now trap car and industrial emissions, making the capital the most polluted major city in the world, and its buildings are sinking rapidly into the soft soil of the lake beds.

Across a band of pine-forested mountains to the east of this valley lies the Valley of Toluca (2,580 meters, 8,600 feet above sea level), which is home to the industrial city of the same name. To the north, the broad plain of the Bajío gradually drops to the arid hills and deserts of Northern Mexico. In the opposite direction, east across the snow-topped volcanoes of Popocatépetl and Iztaccíhuatl extends the Valley of Puebla (2,100 meters, 7,000 feet above sea level), which has been a center of human civilization for over a millennium. Due south of Mexico City lies the Valley of Morelos, 600 meters or 2,000 feet below the capital, and always warmer and more humid, attracting Mexico's rulers since Aztec times.

Facts for the Traveler

Getting There

By Air

The capital's Benito Juárez International Airport is served by direct flights from nearly every city in Mexico. Aeromexico and Mexicana are the two national airlines. Most large cities in North America also have flights to Mexico City, including Atlanta, Charlotte (North Carolina), Chicago, Cincinnati, Cleveland, Dallas, Denver, Houston, Los Angeles, Memphis, Miami, New York, Orlando, Philadelphia, San Antonio, San Diego, San Francisco, San José (California), San Juan (Puerto Rico), Toronto and Tucson. Of the US airlines, Continental serves the most Mexican cities. From the rest of the world, direct international flights to Mexico City originate in Amsterdam, Buenos Aires, Caracas, Guatemala City, Havana, Lima, London, Madrid, Moscow, Panama City, Paris, Rio de Janeiro, San José (Costa Rica), Santiago (Chile), Sao Paulo and Tokyo.

After leaving customs, most travelers will want to continue by taxi to their final destination (the Terminal Aérea Metro station is also right across the street). To take the official airport taxi, with relatively low rates, exit at either end of the long terminal building, where you can purchase a ticket at a window and hop in one of the yellow taxis with the airplane symbol on the side. Over the last few years, a group of aggressive, unofficial airport taxis have pitched camp at the terminal. The worst of their abuses seems to have abated, although they still regularly overcharge.

By Car

All roads in Mexico eventually lead to Mexico City. The main highways into the capital are Mexico 95 from Cuernavaca, Mexico 15 from Toluca, Mexico 57 from Querétaro, Mexico 85 from Pachuca and Mexico 150 from Puebla.

If you are thinking of driving your own car to Mexico City, you must buy Mexican insurance before you cross the border (difficult in the south). Mexican authorities have recently attacked the problem of people selling US-bought cars in Mexico by insisting that drivers prove that they have no intention of selling their vehicle. You can either do this by posting a bond at the border (bonding agencies here will cover this for one to two per cent of the car's assessed value) or by making a sworn statement and paying a US$12 fee (credit card only) at the Banco Nacional del Ejército counter in the customs office. Before you attempt to cross, make sure that all your documentation is in order. The owner of the car must be in the vehicle at all times when travelling in Mexico. Automobile permits are valid for 180 days; if you

The Torre Latinoamericana rises beside Bellas Artes Palace

forget to get an extension, the penalties can be huge. You do not need to obtain these permits if you are only driving your car within the 'free zone' along the border.

By Bus

Bus lines arrive from the provinces into one of four bus stations named after the points of the compass. The Central Camionera del Norte serves buses from the north of the country and is located on Eje Central Lázaro Cárdenas at the Metro Autobuses del Norte station. The Central Camionera del Oriente, for Veracruz and other points east, stands just east of Eje 3 Oriente at Metro San Lázaro. Buses from Cuernavaca, Acapulco and other southern destinations arrive at the Central Camionera del Sur at Metro Tasqueña, a block east of Calz de Tlalpan. The western bus station, the Central Camionera del Poniente, for arrivals from Toluca and Michoacán, lies a few blocks west of the Periférico near Metro Observatorio.

By Train

Mexico City's Buenavista railway station is the terminus of all the main train lines; these originate at Mexicali, Guadalajara, Ciudad Juárez, Piedras Negras, Veracruz, Mérida, Oaxaca and Uruapán. The station is located just off Insurgentes Norte, a block north of Eje 1 Norte and five blocks west of the Guerrero Metro station.

Visas

United States and Canadian residents need a passport, birth certificate, voter's registration card or Green Card to enter Mexico. Except for the French, who need a visa, all citizens of Western European countries only need a passport to enter Mexico. Citizens of the former Eastern Bloc nations need a visa. On arrival at Mexican immigration, you must present a filled-out tourist card (available at the larger border crossings, on planes and with most travel agents, always *free*) to the officer. These are normally stamped for a 30-day stay. If you need more time, ask for longer, although this is not always granted. You can get extensions at the Secretaría de Gobernación, Dir Gen de Servicios Migratorios office (first floor) at 19 Calle Albañíles, Colonia 20 de Noviembre in Mexico City or at international airports. Do not lose your tourist card, because this causes hassles when you are trying to leave the country. There is a departure tax of US$12 on international flights and US$4 on domestic flights.

Customs

You are allowed to bring into Mexico three liters of alcohol, one carton of cigarettes (or 50 cigars or one kilogram of tobacco), US$80 worth of gifts, 12 rolls of film and—for personal use only—electronic gadgetry like a portable computer, camera, radio or television. At customs in international airports, you are asked to push a button, and if the light turns red (not often), your luggage is cursorily searched. At smaller border crossings, the search depends on the whim of the customs agents. Bear in mind that on re-entering the United States, the importation of endangered species products, such as tortoise shell and black coral, is prohibited.

Climate

Mexico City and the surrounding states are a year-round destination, although some seasons are definitely more pleasant than others. Most tourists visit during the winter dry season between late October and May. During this period, the city and the surrounding Central Highlands are dry and mild; daytime temperatures usually hover around 20°C (68°F) with occasional cold snaps. Unfortunately, cold weather causes temperature inversions that trap pollution in the Valley of Mexico. There are occasional snowfalls up on the volcanoes and in the mountains west of Toluca. At the end of the dry season, between April and mid-June, Mexico City is often hot (reaching 32°C, 90°F), dry and polluted. During the summer rainy season, the city is flooded by daily downpours (that also wash the pollution from the air) and even the money becomes damp and clammy. Bring a sweater and rain gear at this time, and watch out for the bottomless puddles. Mexico City is prettiest in late October and November when the rains have ended and the vegetation is still green (and there are the fewest tourists).

Clothing

Mexicans prefer to dress more formally than Americans or Europeans. Outside of resort areas like Acapulco and Cancún, where attitudes are much more relaxed, men wear long pants and, for business, suits or jackets and ties. Many of the better restaurants in the big cities will require you to wear at least a jacket for dinner. Women also dress more modestly than their northern counterparts; slacks are acceptable but short shorts, mini-skirts and belly-exposing outfits are thought fit only for prostitutes.

Foreign women so dressed will expose themselves to the full onslaught of Mexican machismo. Mexicans take these customs particularly seriously with regard to religion; unacceptably dressed tourists will not be allowed into churches.

Health

Health is a major concern of visitors to Mexico. By following a few rules, you can avoid the most common trip-ruining ailments. On first arriving in Mexico City (altitude 2,278 meters, 7,493 feet) go slowly for the first day or two and restrict your alcohol intake until you become acclimatized to the height.

The tap water in most Mexican towns and cities, including Mexico City, is impure. You can avoid stomach problems by drinking and brushing your teeth with bottled *agua purificada* ('purified water'), which is available in supermarkets, discount stores, hotel gift shops and some pharmacies throughout Mexico. Many big resort-type hotels have their own water purification systems that produce safe tap water. If there is no other water available, the water from the hot water tap is usually heated long enough to kill the germs. Most of the better restaurants also purify their water, but if you have any doubts drink soda or mineral water (*agua mineral*) without ice (*sin hielo*).

Contaminated water also affects the food you eat, because it is washed in it. Raw unpeeled vegetables, salads, fruits you have not peeled yourself and all food from street stands and cheap restaurants should be avoided. You can also get many diseases from unpasteurized milk and ice cream. The symptoms of the most common intestinal complaint, Montezuma's Revenge or *La Turista*, are cramps and diarrhea (locals, particularly children, actually suffer from this more than tourists). If you have a mild case, stop eating and keep up your water (or apple juice) intake, perhaps with a little sugar and salt added, until it is over. In more severe cases or if you have to travel, medication should be added to the fluid regimen. Yoghurt is now considered counter-productive. Avoid over-medication; use drugs like Pepto-Bismol or Imodium unless the cramps become acute, when Lomotil-type medications are recommended. For anything worse, you should see a doctor as soon as possible.

The combination of Mexico City's altitude and severe pollution may lead to lung problems for those with chronic respiratory disorders. High ozone and pollutant levels can irritate the breathing tracts and open the way for bacteria to infect the lungs with bronchitis and other diseases. If you are susceptible to these disorders, consult your doctor before leaving and travel with a supply of antibiotics. Most Mexico City newspapers carry daily pollution reports that break the smog level down by zones. Known as IMECA, or 'Metropolitan Air Quality Index', this lists the level of

(*above*) Cortés and La Malinche, *depicted by José Clemente Orozco;*

(*below*) Diego Rivera's history of Mexico, National Palace

four major pollutants: ozone, sulphur dioxide, nitrogen dioxide and carbon monoxide. Zero to 100 is satisfactory, 101–200 not satisfactory, 201–300 bad and 301–500 is very bad. As the smog levels rise above 100, usually led by the ozone count, various stages of alert, including closing factories and sending schoolchildren home, go into effect. Midday to early afternoon is usually the worst. Unfortunately, most tourists do not listen to Mexican radio, so they learn about it the next day when they come down with headaches and sore throats. Due to traffic levels and prevailing winds, Mexico City's central and southeastern zones, including San Angel and Coyoacán, are generally the most polluted. English-speaking doctors are found in all the resorts and major cities; ask at the desk of any large hotel. For emergencies, and on weekends, your best bet is the ABC hospital, officially known as the American British Cowdray Hospital, at Calle Sur 138 in Colonia Las Américas near Metro Observatorio. Mexican pharmacies are well stocked with drugs, many manufactured by American and European firms, and you do not need a prescription for most of them.

Visitors planning to travel into the hinterlands should be inoculated for typhoid and bring along anti-malarial tablets if traveling rough along the Gulf Coast. Cholera has recently spread to Mexico from South America. The AIDS epidemic has hit Mexico's big cities; condoms are widely available.

Money

Mexico's currency is the Mexican peso (N$). At the time of former president Salinas, the peso to dollar exchange rate had stabilized at about three pesos to one US dollar. Just after Ernesto Zedillo took office, however, the peso suffered a strong devaluation, with the rate finally settling at N$8.50 to the dollar. This event is popularly known as 'December's error', since President Zedillo's administration began in that month, in 1994.

Transportation

By Air

The two main national airlines, Mexicana and Aeromexico, serve nearly every Mexican city and resort area. Mexico City is the main hub, so from here there are direct flights to every destination in the country. Puebla and Toluca also have airports, but they are so close to the capital that most people prefer to fly into Mexico City.

By Car

Travelling by car in Mexico has its pleasures and its perils. A car allows you to delve into many of the country's nooks and crannies and see marvels you would otherwise be unable to reach. Rental cars are expensive, but you can generally save money if you make the reservation outside Mexico. Remember that the cost of the insurance and a 15 per cent tourist tax are added to the basic rental rates. Gasoline is less expensive here than it is in the United States and, as a means to fight pollution, is only sold as unleaded and diesel. Pemex sells two varieties of unleaded gasoline—Magna Sin and the more expensive, higher-octane Premium. Check that the pump is set at zero before they start filling and that you receive the correct change after paying.

Due to the pollution, authorities have restricted the days that you can drive in Mexico City; they are based on the last number of your license plate (foreign plates are not exempt). On Monday the forbidden final numbers are five or six, Tuesday seven or eight, Wednesday three or four, Thursday one or two, and Friday nine or zero. However, this does not apply if your car bears a type-0 sticker—which indicates that it has a less-polluting engine—on either the side or rear window. All license plates may drive on Saturdays and Sundays. On days of particularly bad pollution, the forbidden days may jump to two a week; keep an eye on the papers. If you are caught, your vehicle will be impounded and you will have to pay a heavy fine. Also, remember to fasten your seatbelt. It is now mandatory.

A book could be written about the perils of the Mexican highway. The roads are overcrowded, potholed, narrow and with no shoulders. Mexican drivers usually enter a road first and look second. Instead of lights and stop signs, Mexicans use *topes*, speed bumps, which come in the following varieties: metal bumps, single ridge, washboard, washboard between two ridges, and the dreaded reverse *tope*, which is actually an invisible ditch that scrapes the bottom off your car. Many Mexican policemen supplement their salaries through traffic fines, and tourists are considered rich pickings. If you are in such a shake-down situation, you have two alternatives: the one most commonly practiced by Mexicans is to *politely* say that you had no idea you were breaking a (non-existent) regulation but you are in a great hurry, is there not some way you could pay a fine right there? Then you agree on a price (not showing your wallet) and make the pay-off. If the idea of paying a bribe offends you and you have a good command of Spanish, take down the policeman's name and number and ask to be taken to the nearest police station, where you can register your complaint (if of course the charge was unjustified). In car accidents, the Mexican practice is to lock up both parties until all claims are settled, even if you have insurance—some people prefer to leave the accident scene first.

Driving at night is not advisable, because those are the hours that *bandidos* roam the roads, and you may also encounter farm animals and drunks asleep on the pavement. When parking in big cities, never leave the car on the streets overnight, unless you want your luggage, battery or your entire car stolen. Hotel parking lots with 24-hour guards are the safest. Mexico's roads are patrolled by the *Angeles Verdes* ('Green Angels'), a free government travelers' aid service that cruises along nearly every Mexican road of any size, at least twice a day. They can perform minor repairs and first aid; they can also call for assistance if necessary.

By Bus

Buses reach nearly every community in Mexico and are generally an inexpensive, fast and reliable way to travel. There are first-, second- and local-class buses; in most cities, all the lines are collected in one central bus station, while in others each line has a separate terminal—sometimes many blocks apart. Mexico City's four terminals serve destinations in the four directions of the compass. The distinctions between first and second class are not always clear. First class has reserved seats and is usually newer, cleaner, air conditioned (sometimes), makes less stops and no unscheduled pick-ups; second class is slower, less expensive and slightly dirtier. The toilets are kept locked, and you have to ask the driver for the key. On long-distance trips there are two drivers; one drives while the other sleeps on a mattress in the luggage compartment. There has been a rash of robberies on late-night buses; travel during the day time if possible. New luxury bus services are now offered by lines like ETN between Mexico City, the Bajío region and Guadalajara. Seats may be more than twice as expensive as regular first class, but the buses feature leg rests, complimentary sodas, uniformed attendants and video monitors that usually show the latest Stallone movies. Mexican bus stations are usually jammed around the holidays; arrive early and be prepared to queue.

By Train

Travelling on the state-run train service, Ferrocarriles Nacionales de Mexico, can be an exercise in frustration. The antiquated rolling stock is slow and frequently breaks down, while buying tickets is sometimes a bureaucratic nightmare. The Copper Canyon train and the luxury-sleeper services between Guadalajara and Monterrey and Mexico City are happy exceptions. Sleeping accommodation includes curtained berths, small private rooms and larger rooms with a private bathroom. Tickets for these should be purchased as far in advance as possible. The best non-sleeper tickets are special first class, with comfortable reclining seats. Thieves frequently work the regular first-class and second-class carriages, particularly at night. The Mérida-Mexico City train has a reputation for running days late.

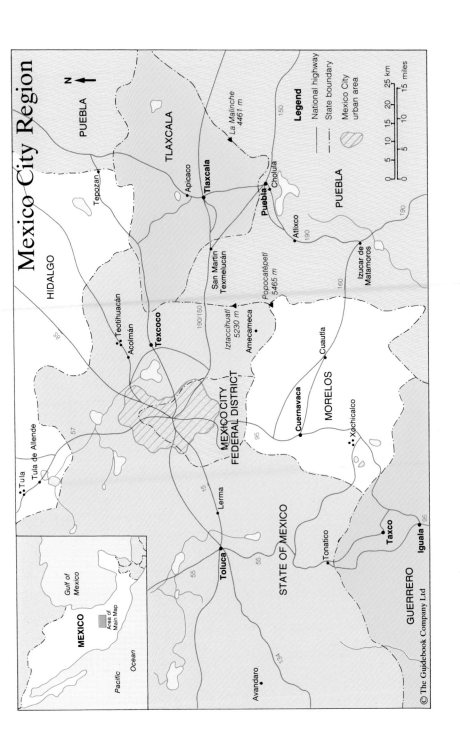

Mexico City Region

N

HIDALGO

PUEBLA

TLAXCALA

Tepozan

Apicaco

Tlaxcala

La Malinche
4461 m

Teotihuacán
Acolmán

Texcoco

San Martín
Texmelucán

Puebla

Cholula

Atlixco

PUEBLA

190

Popocatépetl
5465 m

Izúcar de
Matamoros

Tula
Tula de Allende

57

85

190/150

Iztaccíhuatl
5230 m
Amecameca

MEXICO CITY
FEDERAL DISTRICT

95

160

Cuautla

Cuernavaca

MORELOS

Xochicalco

15

Lerma

Toluca

55

55

STATE OF MEXICO

Tonatico

Taxco

Iguala

95

GUERRERO

134

Avandaro

Legend

— National highway
—·— State boundary
▨ Mexico City
urban area

0   5   10   15   20   25 km

0   5   10   15 miles

MEXICO

Gulf of
Mexico

Area of
Main Map

Pacific
Ocean

© The Guidebook Company Ltd

Communications

Nearly every town and city has a post office, and the bright red mailboxes are widespread. Postal service is slow; letters to the United States often take three weeks. Correos Mexicanos has a reputation for corruption, so you should never send anything valuable by mail, although books and documents are generally considered safe. For fast and reliable package service within Mexico, try one of the long-distance bus lines. International packages should be sent via an overseas courier service like DHL or Federal Express.

Mexico's telephone company, Télmex, had a long-standing reputation for terrible and over-priced service (witness the city's cellular phone explosion), but it was recently purchased by a consortium of national and foreign investors, and service has improved significantly. Many hotels impose exorbitant surcharges on operator-assisted calls; try to self-dial as much as possible. The Mexican government also charges high taxes on all international calls. LADA public phones for both local and long-distance calls require pre-paid phone cards which are available at newsstands and many shops. You may find phones that accept coins, but they are rare. US long-distance companies now have a service to and from Mexico, which lowers rates significantly. The long-distance prefixes are: 01 for calls within Mexico; 001 for the US and Canada; and 00 plus country code for the rest of the world (then dial city code and number). Telegraph services from Telégrafos Nacionales are also available.

Mexico is saturated with newspapers, because the price of newsprint is state-subsidized, the Government buys most of the advertising space, and owning a newspaper can confer great political power (whether they have a significant readership or not is a matter of debate). In all tourist areas you can buy either of the two English-language papers: the hoary *Mexico City News*, or the new *Mexico City Times* which has more US coverage. American papers and magazines like the *New*

Photomontage of La Raza by Hermanos Mayo

York Times, *USA Today*, the *Wall Street Journal*, *Time* and *Newsweek* are available in Sanborn's, in gift shops in the more expensive hotels, and at some downtown Mexico City newsstands. Most big tourist hotels have US television beamed via satellite. The largest national dailies include *El Universal* (independent), *Reforma* (independent), *El Excelsior* (conservative), *El Financero* (financial), *La Prensa* (a lurid tabloid — the most popular), and *La Jornada* (the left-wing bible). *Reforma* and *Metro* (recently launched to compete with La Prensa) are not sold at newsstands, but may be found in many convenience stores, cafeterias, etc., and are also hawked at traffic lights. The magazines *Proceso*, *Epoca*, *Este País* and *Siempre* are the best for in-depth political reporting. The best English-language book store in Mexico City is the American Book Store at 25 Calle Madero near the Alameda; also try Librería Británica at 125 Calle Serapio Rendón and any Sanborn's branch. Guides on where to go and what to do are the local magazines *Tiempo Libre* and *Dónde Ir*, the latter having listings in English.

Time, Measurements and Electricity

Mexico has three time zones, but most of the country runs on US Central Standard Time (six hours behind GMT). The states of Sonora, Sinaloa, Nayarit and Baja California Sur are on Mountain Standard Time (seven hours behind GMT). Baja California Norte falls into a special category, following MST in summer and Pacific Standard Time the rest of the year. Between the first Sunday in April and the last Sunday in October all clocks go forward one hour.

Mexico adheres to the metric system. It also runs on 110 volt AC current with two-pin rectangular plugs, as in the United States. Electrical cords with different-sized prongs will not fit in Mexican plugs, so bring an adapter. Power failures and brown-outs are not uncommon.

Holidays

The most important religious holidays in Mexico are December 10–12, when the Festival of Our Lady of Guadalupe is celebrated throughout the country; Christmas, which begins at least a week before December 25 and continues until the Day of the Three Kings, the traditional time of gift-giving, in early January; and the weeks leading up to Easter, first with Carnival, then with re-enactments of the Passion, and finally Good Friday and Easter itself. Mexico's most unique religious holiday is the

Day of the Dead, the night between November 1 and 2, when Mexicans honor their ancestors by constructing elaborate altars and holding all-night vigils in the graveyards. The Day of the Dead is celebrated throughout Mexico, but the rituals practiced around Cuernavaca and in Xochimilco, south of Mexico City, are particularly famous.

Legal National Holidays

January 1	New Year	September 16	Independence Day
February 5	Constitution Day	November 20	Revolution Day
March 21	Benito Juárez Birthday	December 25	Christmas
May 1	Labor Day		

Here are a handful of historical events celebrated in cities and towns across Mexico:

Cholula	Festival of Our Lady of Remedies	September 8
Cuernavaca	Flower Festival	May 2
Cuernavaca	Festival of the Virgin Mary's Birth	September 15
Mexico City	Fiesta in the Plaza of Three Cultures, Tlatelolco	Sunday after St James' Day
Mexico City	Passion re-enactment, Iztapalapa	Good Friday
Mexico City	Our Lady of Guadalupe, the Basilica	December 12
Puebla	Day of Victory Over the French	May 5
Xochimilco	Passion Week festivals	week before Easter

Tourist Information

In Mexico City, the Department of Tourism main offices are located at 172 Av Masaryk near Reforma. Abroad, there are Mexican Government Tourism Offices in New York (405 Park Avenue, Suite 1402, New York, NY 10022), Washington DC (1911 Pennsylvania Avenue, Washington, DC 20006), Chicago (70 Lake Street, Suite 1413, Chicago, IL 60601), Houston (2707 North Loop West, Suite 450, Houston, TX 77008), Los Angeles (10100 Santa Monica Boulevard, Suite 224, Los Angeles, CA 90067), Toronto (2 Bloor Street West, Suite 1801, Toronto, Ontario H3B 3M9), London (60/61 Trafalgar Square, London WC2N 5DS), Madrid (126 Calle Velasquez, Madrid 28006), Paris (4 rue Notre-Dame Des Victoires, 75002 Paris), Frankfurt (Wiesen-hüttenplatz 26, D6000 Frankfurt Am Main 1), Rome (Via Barberini 3, 00187 Rome) and Tokyo (2-15-1 Chiyoda-ku, Tokyo 100).

Eating and Drinking

FOOD

Mexican cuisine is one of the finest in the world. Unfortunately, authentic dishes are becoming harder to find due to the influence of fast food, tourists' food prejudices and the levelling of regional differences by modern urban culture. Before the arrival of the Spanish, corn was the staff of life for Mesoamerican civilization. It was usually ground and made into *tortillas*, *tamales* and other breads, or mixed into drinks, flavored gruels and stews. Chilli peppers and salt were the essential seasonings, and a meal without them was considered fasting. The Aztecs, who lived in the middle of an incredibly rich lake environment, ate a wide variety of plant and animal foods, including beans, squash, tomatoes, ducks, fish, frogs, flies, amaranth, chocolate, cactus fruit, dried algae, mushrooms, fat hairless dogs and, yes, human meat, usually in a stew with tomatoes and chillies (probably for ritual purposes only). Cooking fat was unknown, but they did eat sweets made from maguey syrup or honey. Motecuhzoma's meals usually included over a hundred dishes (as a deity, he ate alone). The Mayas of Southern Mexico had a similar diet but added tropical gourmet items like iguana and monkey meat (for the élite, at least). *Tamales*, corn meal wrapped in corn husks and steamed, were a Maya specialty, and they also invented the *pibil*, a stone-lined oven in which food was sealed and baked until tender.

When the conquistadors arrived, they found an incredible variety of new fruits and types of wild game. Not exactly gourmets, they learned to enjoy some of the local cuisine, but they found the lack of fat and oil unbearable. After the Conquest, they imported pigs, cattle, sheep, wine, wheat, cheese, olive oil, herrings, European spices and sugar to reconstruct their Spanish diet. Nevertheless, the intermingling of cuisines was inevitable; the Spanish royalty were soon sipping chocolate drinks, and Yucatecan Indians discovered the joys of pork cooked in their pibils. The next great influence on Mexican cuisine began when Napoleon's troops invaded in 1862; French cooking became the height of fashion and remained so under the Francophile

Modern Aztec dancers

regime of Porfirio Díaz. In this century, it is American fast food—hamburgers everywhere—that has transformed Mexican diets. Today many other cuisines have begun to appear in the big cities, like Italian pastas and even sushi.

Each of Mexico's regions has a distinctive cuisine, and a trip dedicated to sampling their dishes can be rewarding and delectable. The Mexico City area and the surrounding states have the most clearly Aztec and Spanish food. *Mole* sauces, which were invented in Puebla and are made from ground chilli, chocolate and spices, are delicious on chicken and other meats. The Mexican national dish, *chiles en nogada*, is a perfect example of the Aztec-Spanish blend. This was supposedly invented in 1821 by a Puebla chef for General Iturbide, who was making his victorious march to the capital after ejecting the Spanish. The chillies are breaded peppers (Aztec) stuffed with ground meat and pine nuts and then covered with a sweet walnut sauce (Spanish). The chef garnished the dish with pomegranate seeds and sprigs of parsley, which, together with the 'alabaster' of the walnut sauce, make up the colors of the Mexican flag.

In Mexico City's restaurants, you can also find specialties from every other state in Mexico. Michoacán is famous for its sweets, like *chongos*, a sugary curd made from rennet. The states of Jalisco, Colima and Nayarit to the northwest are known for their *carnitas* (roast meats) and *pozole*, a stew made from hominy and tripe and other meats. In Oaxaca and Chiapas they add more sugar and spices like cloves and cinnamon to their *moles; tamales* are also their specialty. The Gulf states are famous for their seafood, like *huauchinango a la veracruzana*—red snapper with tomatoes, chillies, olives and capers. This is also the region with the greatest Caribbean influence. Yucatán has the most distinctive cuisine. The warming *achiote* powder is the favorite seasoning; the fiery, mouth-watering *habanero* chilli accompanies every meal; and many dishes are still cooked to perfect tenderness in the *pibil* ovens. In the north they serve cowboy food: corn tortillas are replaced by wider flour tortillas, and the regional specialties are 'cowboy-style' bean stew, steak, *chorizo* sausage and roast goat. There are also many special dishes for holidays, like sweet, rich *pan de muerto* ('bread of death') for the Day of the Dead and *tortas de camarón*, a kind of freshwater shrimp cake made at Easter in Mexico City and Puebla.

GUIDE TO A MEXICAN MENU

HUEVOS	EGGS
Fritos	Fried
Revueltos	Scrambled
Rancheros	Fried, with a chilli and tomato sauce
Mexicanos	Scrambled with chillies, onions and tomatoes
Machacado con huevos	Scrambled with beef jerky

Banana dancer, Agustín Casasola

TORTILLAS

Chilaquiles	Casserole of tortillas, sometimes with chicken, in a green chilli sauce
Enchiladas	Soft tortillas filled and covered with red or green chilli sauce
Tacos	Tortillas with meat
Chalupas	Tortilla boats, usually with a meat and bean filling
Tostadas	Fried and garnished tortillas
Quesadillas	Tortilla turnovers filled with cheese and fried
Quesadillas con huitlacoche	Quesadillas with corn fungus
Panuchos	Tortillas stuffed with beans and fried
Gorditas	Fat tortillas with a bean filling and a topping
Burritos	Filled flour tortillas

ANTOJITOS OR BOTANAS	APPETIZERS
Carnitas	Pieces of browned pork
Guacamole	Avocado blended with onions, chillies, coriander and lime juice
Tamales	Corn meal and meat steamed in a corn husk
Ensalada de nopalitos	Nopal cactus salad
Queso fundido	Melted cheese served with tortillas
Seviche	Marinated raw fish with chillies and onions
Frijoles charros	Beans in broth
Frijoles refritos	Refried beans
Cebollitas asadas	Roast spring onions with lime

SOPAS	SOUPS
Caldo de pollo	Chicken soup
Sopa de lima	Lime soup with chicken and tortillas
Caldo de queso	Cheese broth
Caldo tlalpeño	Vegetable soup with chicken and chick peas
Sopa de elote	Corn soup
Menudo Norteño	Tripe stew
Pozole	Hominy stew with tripe or pork
Caldo de pescado	Fish stew

POLLO	CHICKEN
Pollo con mole poblano o verde	With brown or green *mole*

Pollo en pipián rojo	In a red sesame seed sauce
Pollo pibil	Baked in a pibil oven with *achiote* seasoning
Pollo en escabeche	With onions, chillies and vinegar
Pechuga de pollo	Chicken breasts
Pollo Norteño	Marinated and grilled

CARNE	MEAT
Carne asada a la Tampiqueña	Roast meat with assorted appetizers— including *quesadillas* and *guacamole*
Puntas de filete a la Mexicana	Beef with tomatoes and onions
Albóndigas	Meatballs
Chorizo	Spicy sausage
Puerco en mole verde	Pork in green *mole* sauce
Loma de puerco en adobo	Pork in a rich red chilli sauce
Chiles rellenos de picadillo	Chillies stuffed with pork
Cochinita pibil	Pork baked in a *pibil* oven
Carne con chile colorado	Meat in red chilli sauce
Lengua	Tongue
Cabrito	Roast baby goat

MARISCOS	SEAFOOD
Pescado relleno	Stuffed fish
Pescado al mojo de ajo	Fried fish with garlic
Huachinango	Red snapper
Camarones	Shrimp
Langosta	Lobster
Jaibas rellenas	Stuffed crab
Ostiones	Oysters

POSTRES	DESSERTS
Flan	Egg custard
Pay de queso	Cheese pie
Pay de nuez	Pecan pie
Crepas con cajeta	Crepes with sweet goat's milk syrup
Arroz con leche	Rice pudding
Buñuelos	Sweet fritters
Pastel	Cake
Guayabas	Guava in syrup
Helado	Ice cream

DRINK

As with food, the political and cultural history of Mexico can be traced through what people drank. Chocolate was the favorite non-alcoholic beverage for the pre-Columbian Indians, and the main alcoholic drink was *pulque*, the sour, mildly fermented juice of the maguey cactus. Despite their blood-thirsty practices, the Aztecs were remarkably puritanical; drunkeness was savagely punished, and only senior citizens were allowed to freely imbibe *pulque*. After the Conquest, the Indians turned to *pulque* to forget their troubles and alcoholism was widespread. The Spanish, who preferred wine and *aguardiente* (diluted raw rum or other alcohol), discovered that the juice of the agave cactus (or maguey) could be distilled into a clear liquor that packed a hefty punch; *mezcal* was born. The Spanish settlers later imported grape vines, but wine production was forbidden because vineyard owners back in Spain complained about the competition. One of the reasons that Miguel Hidalgo started the Insurgency was that colonial authorities had destroyed his vines. In the late 19th century, Porfirio Díaz encouraged the importation of German beer-making technology, and many excellent breweries sprang up across the country.

Today *pulque* production, which is confined to the central highlands, has fallen off sharply, and the *pulquerías* that remain are generally dirty and dangerous. This is a shame because scientists have discovered that *pulque* has many nutritive properties. The liquors of choice are rum, *tequila*—produced only in Jalisco—and *mezcal*, which is made in Northern Mexico, Oaxaca and Chiapas (check to see that the *mezcal* bottle says '100% agave'; if not it is just flavored alcohol). The most common cocktail is a *cuba libre*—equal parts rum, soda water and cola with lime. Popular ways of drinking *tequila* and *mezcal* are straight with a beer or with a *sangrita* chaser (blood orange juice, tomato juice and chilli powder) or in a cocktail like a margarita. Mexican breweries produce many excellent beers. The main national brands are Superior, Dos Equis, Carta Blanca, Corona, Tecate, Bohemia and Negra Modelo, and you can also buy often better regional brands like León and Montejo from Yucatán or Pacífica from Mazatlán. Mexico's wine industry has been struggling ever since the royal ban on vineyards during colonial days. The most renowned vineyards are now just inland from Baja's Pacific coast, near the towns of Tecate and Ensenada (Bodegas de Santo Tomás there is one of the best). Vineyards are also starting production in Zacatecas and Querétaro. The majority of pressings from Mexican grapes go toward making brandy; Domecq is the major brand. Interesting non-alcoholic drinks include *café de olla* (coffee with brown sugar, cinnamon and anise seeds), *horchata* (a sweet rice drink), *aguas de jamaica* (water flavored with hibiscus flowers) and *tamarindo* (tamarind-flavored water).

PULQUE

Pulque, the fermented, mildly alcoholic juice of the spiny maguey plant, is something of a mystery to outsiders. It is not advertised on TV nor sold in restaurants or supermarkets. Movie stars and socialites are not shown drinking it at parties. Its only outlets are *pulquerías*, a type of cantina, usually unmarked and found in the poor residential neighborhoods. The biases of Mexico's middle and upper classes against *pulque* are summarized by Terry's 1909 *Guide to Mexico*:

> The *pulquerías* are usually thronged with bleary-eyed, sodden male and female degenerates, and they are the foci of much of the crime which shames the intelligent element of the capital. Albeit the intoxicating elements of *pulque* are slight, its cheapness (3 to 5 cents a quart) enables the poorest to buy it. The consumers are chiefly the idle and the common laboring classes, to whom it is meat, drink, and a constant stimulus to crime. Thus the very poorest and most ignorant of the city's population—those most in need of education and uplifting—spend 20,000 pesos each day for the 100 or more carloads that come to the city.

When you finally grasp a glass of the milky, slightly fizzy liquid, the mystery may also be why people drink it. *Pulque* has the texture of saliva, a mildly sour flavor and the aftertaste of the sawdust on a bar-room floor the morning after—a yeasty fermenting odor. And yet, it grows on you. And there are signs that the drink may be making a comeback: at a recent rock concert by a top Mexico City band, the auditorium's atmosphere was redolent, not of marijuana or cigarette smoke, but of *pulque's* tell-tale bouquet.

Pulque was not always synonymous with degeneracy and backwardness. Mexico's pre-Conquest inhabitants considered the maguey, of which there are over 400 species, the 'plant of the marvels', and turned its parts into everything from roofing to needles and medicine. Maguey fiber textiles dated 8000 BC were found in a cave in the northern state of Coahuila, and

continues

many of the Aztec codices were made from maguey paper. *Pulque*, called *iztac octli* or 'white wine' by the Aztecs, was perhaps the maguey's most revered product. According to Aztec mythology, *pulque* was invented by the goddess Mayahuel, always shown seated in a maguey plant, who discovered the method of scraping the plant's heart to draw the juice. She served her invention to the other gods and to the principal chiefs but warned that four cups was the limit, a fifth would lead to drunkeness. One chief drank the fatal fifth and became so drunk that he threw off his loin cloth and capered around naked! The next day, the shame of him and his people was so great that they moved to the northeast where they quickly earned a reputation as drunkards, entertainers and musicians. Myths like this, as well as repeated maguey symbols in sites like El Tajín, have led anthropologists to theorize that *pulque* was first invented by northeastern groups like the Huastecs or the Otomis.

Pulque also played a part in the downfall of Quetzalcoatl, the great king of Tula. One day when Quetzalcoatl was sick, his enemy, the god Tezcatlipoca, assumed the guise of an old man and approached the king with a bowl of *pulque*, which he claimed was medicine. After many refusals, Quetzalcoatl finally drank the *pulque* and of course became drunk. Later, the shame for being drunk was so great he abandoned Tula to his enemies and embarked on his great exodus. In the often puritanical Aztec society, the lesson of Quetzalcoatl, to avoid overindulgence, was reinforced with shocking harshness: public drunkenness could be punishable by death. Those allowed to get drunk were high priests, old men and women (there blood 'runs cold') and, on certain ritual occasions, everybody else.

The process of making *pulque*, the one taught by Mayahuel, has hardly changed in over a millennium. As well-protected as a cactus, the maguey is an unrelated plant with thick green spikes radiating from its heart. *Pulque* is produced from one of six species found exclusively in the Central Highlands around Mexico City (tequila and mezcal are produced from completely different species). The plant has a life span of 7–12 years, at the end of which it sends up a tall flowering shoot and dies. When the *tlachiquero* ('scraper') sees that the plant is about to flower, he 'castrates' it by cutting out the flowering part at the top of the heart. This cavity is left to sit for a few months while the plant continues to build up sap, called *aguamiel* ('honey water'). Then the cavity is cleaned and scraped, and the *aguamiel* begins to collect at the bottom. The *tlachiquero* harvests the juice, perhaps two liters a day—at dawn and dusk by sucking up into a long hollow gourd called an *acocote*. From the field it is taken to the *tinacal* or processing plant for fermentation. The *aguamiel* naturally contains the bacteria that activate fermentation and produce alcohol, so the process may have already begun. The fresh *aguamiel* is usually added to a 'starter' of already fermented *pulque* and is ready to drink in one to two weeks. *Pulque* must be sent to the *pulquerías* quickly, because the fermentation process never stops and the drink can go bad in a matter of days.

After the Conquest, *pulque* was desacralized, the prohibitions against it disappeared and the demoralized Indians turned to drink as a means of drowning their despair at the collapse of their universe. The colonial administration was torn between greed—*pulque* taxes were the fourth largest source of revenue—and concern that their Indian labor force was drinking itself to death. In 1672, the first pulque regulations were put into effect, severely limiting the number of *pulquerías*, which were usually mere tents set up in the marketplace. Some of the rules, like no mixing of men and women or serving *pulque* in restaurants, remain in effect today. In contrast, there were relatively few restrictions on bars and cantinas serving beer, wine and brandy. Whenever business slumped, brewers and vintners would demand that the government enforce the *pulque* regulations to the letter of the law. Because their main customers were the lower classes, *pulquería* owners had little political leverage.

The period between independence in 1821 and the 1910 Revolution was the last golden age of *pulque*. The colonial laws and heavy taxation were abolished and *pulquerías* flourished. With the opening up of train lines to the maguey growing regions during the Porfiriato, transportation to the city became far more efficient. *Pulque* barons, particularly in the state of Hidalgo, built huge and elegant haciendas to manufacture the drink; fortunes were made. In the capital, *pulquerías* were not squalid dives anymore; they became important meeting places for the urban élite, including politicians and artists. Their façades were decorated with bright, cartoonish murals, and the interiors were wood panelled and gleamed with as many shiny fixtures as a fancy cantina. *Pulquerías'* names were often as colorful as their décor: The Wandering Jew, Remembrances of the Future, The Dinosaurs' Drinking Trough, Long Distance Cannon and With You Until Death. The

continues

pulquería opposite the Chamber of Deputies was called The Recreation of Those Across the Street.

The Revolution disrupted the *pulque* industry along with every other sector of Mexican society; however, *pulque* has never recovered. During President Lázaro Cárdenas' campaign to bring Mexican agriculture into the modern era, yearly cash crops and modern farming methods were emphasized and traditional peasant ways, including tending the slow growing maguey, were seen as backward. In the cities, 'American' and 'modern' were the watchwords; beer and cocktails became the drinks of choice, and *pulque* was again seen as low and in 'bad taste'. Industrialization and the chaos in agriculture led peasants to migrate to the cities, particularly the capital, looking for factory work. Between 1930 and 1970, the number of maguey workers dropped 57 per cent, and the number of *pulquerías* has also steadily declined.

In the 1960s, when the government saw that rural Mexico was being abandoned and the loss of maguey plants was leading to erosion and desertification, they began a sporadic campaign to support the *pulque* industry. During their investigations into the uses of the drink, scientists discovered that *pulque* is extremely nutritious. The saying that *pulque* is 'only one step from being meat' is true. It contains significant amounts of Vitamin C and the B Complex vitamins, as well as amino acids and traces of Vitamins D and E. Indians on a poverty-level diet who drink *pulque* do not suffer from a number of diseases caused by malnutrition. Researchers attempted to widen *pulque*'s market and spread its nutritional value by canning the drink, but the resultant beverage apparently did not taste good and the project was cancelled. Since then the government seems to have given up. Indeed, *pulque* has become so marginalized that it is nearly impossible to find the past decade's statistics on the industry.

Nevertheless, *pulque* lives, if on the fringes of Mexican society, and with a little effort visitors can try the mythic beverage. A good place to start is the Plaza Garibaldi, where La Hermosa Hortencia is one of the few *pulquerías* accustomed to handling the tourist trade. Here you can start with a *blanco* ('white'), which is straight *pulque*, and then move on to the many flavored *pulques*, called *curados*, including pineapple, peanut, pistachio and almond flavors. The bartender, called the *jicarero*, generally clad in rubber boots, ladles the drink from wooden barrels or plastic trash cans (easier to clean) behind the bar. Traditionally, there is a vast range of glass sizes, from a small cup to the multi-liter, but most *pulquerías* today use only quarter-, half- and full-liter glasses. The more adventurous, Spanish-speaking visitor will want to try one of the many, far less expensive neighborhood *pulque-rías* that dot the old residential quarters around the center. These generally are divided into a *Sala de Mujeres* ('women's room') about the size of a closet and a much more spacious accommodation for the men. Women may also be allowed here, but it might be assumed that they are of ill re-pute. Some *pulquerías*, particularly in the poorer neighborhoods, accurately reflect Terry's description in that they attract terminal *pulque* bums and fights. You can usually judge a *pulque's* atmosphere within seconds from a quick peek in the door. Every *pulquería* also sells the drink to go, if you provide the container; a liter and a half, which is a lot for one person, generally runs less than US$1.

Before you indulge too deeply in the world of *pulque*, you should remember the story of Quetzalcoatl. If you become too fond of that fifth cup, you might become like the narrator of a traditional ditty, 'The Song of Pulque', which, roughly translated, goes:

> This is the song of *pulque*,
> And now I'm going to sing it to you.
> I composed it last night
> On leaving the *tinacal*.
>
> [Chorus]
> Ay! Ay! Ay! Ay! Aaaaaay!
> We want more *pulque*!
> With parties and *pulque*,
> We'll start the day,
> We'll start the day....
> [Repeat *ad infinitum*]

Crafts

Visitors interested in crafts will find an overflowing bounty in Mexico. Almost every major city has a government-operated crafts store that usually has the lowest prices and highest quality merchandise. With the exception of Day of the Dead paraphernalia, Mexico City is not known for its locally made crafts. However, it has many stores selling the highest-quality goods from the rest of the country. Among the crafts items available are silver and gold jewelry, ceramics, textiles (from clothes to blankets and rugs), leather, lacquerware, musical instruments, hammocks, baskets, hats, toys, onyx, masks, furniture, copperware, tiles and copies of pre-Columbian artefacts. The most important silver jewelry manufacturing town in the world is Taxco, where literally hundreds of dealers offer incredible bargains. Puebla is the center of tile-making, and nearby Cholula has been renowned for the quality of its ceramics since pre-Hispanic times. Toluca has an enormous and renowned Friday market that attracts Indian craftspeople from throughout Central Mexico. Further afield, Michoacán is perhaps the richest crafts center, producing wooden furniture, clothing, guitars, green pineapple-shaped pots, wooden masks, lacquerware and copper. Oaxaca is known for its blankets and rugs, wooden animal carvings, green and black

Cantinflas takes from the rich and gives to the poor;
Diego Rivera mosaic on the Teatro Insurgentes

pottery, and baskets. For textiles, look for goods from Chiapas, which is famous for its Indian weavers. Yucatán's claims to fame are its traditional *huipiles* (blouses) and excellent hammocks.

Mexican crafts

Mexico City is filled with crafts stores. A good place to start is the Alameda. Housed in an old church opposite the Juárez monument, the **Museo de Artes y Industrias Populares** (44 Av Juárez) has a large and excellent display of inexpensive folk crafts, including toys, textiles and silver jewelry. Unfortunately it is now closed for renovation. **FONART**, a block west of the Alameda at 89 Av Juárez, sells ceramics, textiles and glassware. On the second floor are staged temporary exhibitions highlighting one region of Mexico. In the opposite direction, **Victor Artes Populares Mexicanes**, a half block east of the Alameda at 10 Av Madero, is a small and inexpensive crafts shop which sells a wide array of items not found in more touristy markets. If you head four blocks south of the park on Calle Dolores, you come to the **San Juan Artisan's Market**, with two floors of shops selling textiles, jewelry, leather and ceramics. Bus tours are steered here; consequently the prices are high and the goods a little less authentic looking. The **Mercado de Artesanías de la Ciudadela**, three blocks east at the corner of Calles E Pugibet and Balderas, is slightly less expensive but sells much the same wares as San Juan. Another area rich in crafts stores is the Zona Rosa. Calle Londres has a branch of the **FONART** (136) and a number of good private shops, including **Artesanos de México** at 117. The neighborhood is also known for its silver and jewelry stores; they carry the highest quality and their prices reflect it. Down south in the San Angel neighborhood, every Saturday an old mansion on the Plaza San Jacinto becomes the **Bazar Sábado**, with dozens of craftspeople making and selling their wares.

End of the Road

The end of the journey impended. Great fields stretched on both sides of us; a noble wind blew across the occasional immense tree groves and over old missions turning salmon pink in the late sun. The clouds were close and huge and rose. "Mexico City by dusk!" We'd made it, a total of nineteen hundred miles from the afternoon yards of Denver to these vast and Biblical areas of the world, and now we were about to reach the end of the road.

"Shall we change our insect T-shirts?"

"Naw, let's wear them into town, hell's bells." And we drove into Mexico City.

A brief mountain pass took us suddenly to a height from which we saw all of Mexico City stretched out in its volcanic crater below and spewing city smokes and early dusklights. Down to it we zoomed, down Insurgentes Boulevard, straight toward the heart of town at Reforma. Kids played soccer in enormous sad fields and threw up dust. Taxi-drivers overtook us and wanted to know if we wanted girls. No, we didn't want girls now. Long, ragged adobe slums stretched out on the plain; we saw lonely figures in the dimming alleys. Soon night would come. Then the city roared in and suddenly we were passing crowded cafés and theaters and many lights. Newsboys yelled at us. Mechanics slouched by, barefoot, with wrenches and rags. Mad barefoot Indian drivers cut across us and surrounded us and tooted and made frantic traffic. The noise was incredible. No mufflers are used on Mexican cars. Horns are batted with glee continual. "Whee!" yelled Dean. "Look out!" He staggered the car through the traffic and played with everybody. He drove like an Indian. He got on a circular glorietta drive on Reforma Boulevard and rolled around it with its eight spokes shooting cars at us from all directions, left, right, izquierda, dead ahead, and yelled and jumped for joy. "This is traffic I've always dreamed of! Everybody goes!" An ambulance came balling through. American ambulances dart and weave through traffic with siren blowing; the great world-wide Fellahin Indian ambulances merely come through at eighty miles an hour in the city streets, and everybody just has to get out of the way and they don't pause for anybody or any circumstances and fly straight through. We saw it reeling out of sight on skittering wheels in the breaking-up moil of dense downtown traffic. The drivers were Indians. People, even old ladies, ran for buses that never stopped. Young Mexico City businessmen made bets and ran by squads for buses and athletically jumped them. The bus-drivers were barefoot, sneering and insane, and sat low and squat in T-shirts at the low, enormous wheels. Ikons burned over them. The lights in the buses were brown and greenish, and dark faces were lined on wooden benches.

In downtown Mexico City thousands of hipsters in floppy straw hats and long-lapeled jackets over bare chests padded along the main drag, some of them selling crucifixes and weed in the alleys, some of them kneeling in beat chapels next to Mexican burlesque shows in sheds. Some alleys were rubble, with open sewers, and little doors led to closet-size bars stuck in adobe walls. You had to jump over a ditch to get your drink, and in the bottom of the ditch was the ancient lake of the Aztec. You came out of the bar with your back to the wall and edged back to the street. They served coffee mixed with rum and nutmeg. Mambo blared from everywhere. Hundreds of whores lined themselves along the dark and narrow streets and their sorrowful eyes gleamed at us in the night. We wandered in a frenzy and a dream. We ate beautiful steaks for forty-eight cents in a strange tiled Mexican cafeteria with generations of marimba musicians standing at one immense marimba—also wandering singing guitarists, and old men on corners blowing trumpets. You went by the sour stink of pulque saloons; they gave you a water glass of cactus juice in there, two cents. Nothing stopped; the streets were alive all night. Beggars slept wrapped in advertising posters torn off fences. Whole families of them sat on the sidewalk, playing little flutes and chuckling in the night. Their bare feet stuck out, their dim candles burned, all Mexico was one vast Bohemian camp. On corners old women cut up the boiled heads of cows and wrapped morsels in tortillas and served them with hot sauce on newspaper napkins. This was the great and final wild uninhibited Fellahin-childlike city that we knew we would find at the end of the road. Dean walked through with his arms hanging zombie-like at his sides, his mouth open, his eyes gleaming, and conducted a ragged and holy tour that lasted till dawn in a field with a boy in a straw hat who laughed and chatted with us and wanted to play catch, for nothing ever ended.

Jack Kerouac, On the Road, 1955

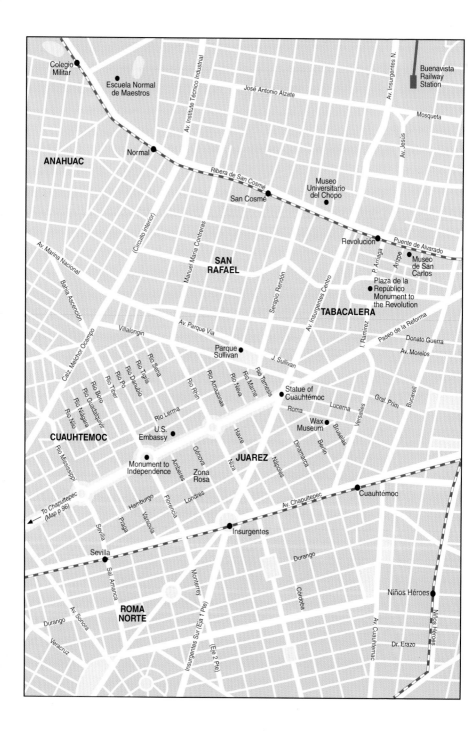

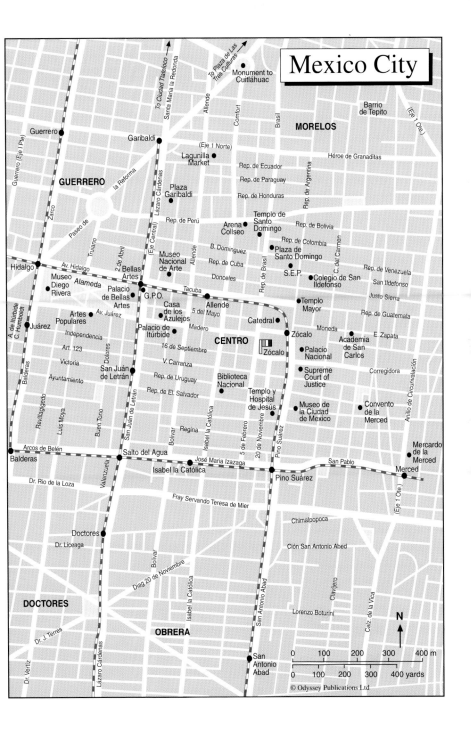

Mexico City

To Ciudad Tlatelolco
Santa María la Redonda
To Plaza de Las Tres Culturas
Monument to Cuitláhuac

Barrio de Tepito

MORELOS

Héroe de Granaditas

Guerrero
Garibaldi

(Eje 1 Norte)

Lagunilla Market

Rep. de Ecuador
Rep. de Paraguay
Rep. de Honduras

Eje 1 Ote

Guerrero (Eje 1 Pte)

GUERRERO

la Reforma

Paseo de

Zarco

2 de Abril

Truijano

Lázaro Cárdenas
(Eje Central)

Plaza Garibaldi

Rep. de Perú

Allende

Comfort

Brasil

Rep. de Argentina

Arena Coliseo

Templo de Santo Domingo

Rep. de Bolivia

Rep. de Colombia

Plaza de Santo Domingo

C. del Carmen

Rep. de Venezuela
San Ildefonso

Justo Sierra

Hidalgo

Av. Hidalgo

2 de Abril

Bellas Artes

Museo Nacional de Arte

B. Dominguez

Rep. de Cuba

Rep. de Brasil

S.E.P.

Colegio de San Ildefonso

Museo Diego Rivera

Alameda

Palacio de Bellas Artes

G.P.O.

Tacuba

Donceles

Templo Mayor

Rep. de Guatemala

A. de Itúrbide
C. Humboldt

Artes Populares

Av. Juárez

Casa de los Azulejos

Allende

5 de Mayo

Catedral

Moneda

E. Zapata

Juárez

Independencia

Palacio de Itúrbide

Madero

Zócalo

Palacio Nacional

Academia de San Carlos

Corregidora

Anillo de Circunvalación

Art. 123

16 de Septiembre

CENTRO

☐ Zócalo

Supreme Court of Justice

Victoria

Dolores

V. Carranza

Ayuntamiento

San Juan de Letrán

Rep. de Uruguay

Biblioteca Nacional

Museo de la Ciudad de Mexico

Convento de la Merced

Balderas

Revillagigedo

Luis Moya

Buen Tono

San Juan de Letrán

Rep. de El. Salvador

Bolívar

Regina

Isabel la Católica

5 de Febrero

20 de Noviembre

Templo y Hospital de Jesús

Pino Suárez

Mercardo de la Merced

Arcos de Belén

Balderas

Salto del Agua

Valenzuela

Isabel la Católica

José María Izazaga

Isabel la Católica

San Pablo

Merced

Pino Suárez

Dr. Río de la Loza

Fray Servando Teresa de Mier

Chimalpopoca

Ción San Antonio Abed

Doctores

Dr. Liceaga

Bolívar

Diag 20 de Noviembre

Isabel la Católica

San Antonio Abad

Clavijero

Calz. de la Vica

DOCTORES

Dr. J. Terres

Lázaro Cárdenas

OBRERA

Lorenzo Boturini

Dr. Vertiz

San Antonio Abad

Eje 1 Ote

N

0   100   200   300   400 m

0   100   200   300   400 yards

© Odyssey Publications Ltd

Mexico City

Getting Around

Mexico City is enormous, and the sights are so widely spread apart that you need to plan how to get around. All the major hotels have English-speaking tour guides who can show you around in their big American cars. An inexpensive alternative is taxis, which are ubiquitous. They come in shades of yellow, green, and red or orange. The latter are *sitios*, or belong to a taxi stand, and therefore are slightly more costly. These have full-time drivers, whereas the drivers of the yellow and green cabs are often moonlighting from other jobs and do not always know the city well. Recently there has been an upsurge of taxi-related robberies in which drivers pick up fares and then an armed accomplice jumps in to rob the passenger. At night many city residents use only *sitio* or hotel taxis. The cheapest overground way to travel is by bus; these, unfortunately, are slow, crowded and often carry pickpockets. Mini-buses called *combis* or *peseros* ply the same routes as buses, usually between metro stations, for slightly more money and are more comfortable and faster. Fares for taxis, buses and minibuses are set by the government. All taxis must use their meters and, in the case of other vehicles, a fare chart should be posted. After 10pm an additional 20 per cent is charged. Taxis driving beyond the city limits, namely into the State of Mexico, charge double from that point. When visiting downtown you should try a man-powered *bicitaxi*: a cart pulled by a bicycle.

Every visitor should try Mexico City's metro system; with nine lines covering most of the city, it is residents' pride and joy and one of the finest in the world. The tickets are cheap (the fare, N$1.5 at the time of writing, in heavily subsidized by the government. You may also purchase a *planilla*—a set of 30 tickets for N$31—but they sell out very quickly once each fortnight), the stations are clean and the trains run quietly on rubber wheels. During rush hours the crush can be oppressive; this is also prime time for pickpockets, so watch your bags and wallets and beware of anyone deliberately blocking your way. Like the Moscow subway, many metro stations are tourist attractions in their own right. Murals grace the walls of the Universidad and Tacubaya stops, among others; Metro La Raza has a 'Tunnel of Science' with museum exhibitions; Pino Suárez possesses its own Aztec temple; a diorama of Tenochtitlán may be seen in the Zócalo station; and so on. Many other stations, like Chapultepec and Hidalgo, also house malls where you can buy everything from tacos to the latest hit record. Street vendors, a product of the country's economic crisis, sometimes clog the walkways of the station, making it hard for crowds of pedestrians to pass. The city government is now trying to dislodge them, causing occasionally bloody confrontations.

Navigating Mexico City, particularly the out-of-the-way places, requires a good map. The best are the *Guía Pronto* and *Guía Roji* city atlases (the latter, with a glued binding, tends to fall apart quickly). Mexico City is so large and has so many streets (almost 45,000) that street names are often duplicated. If you are looking for a street, particularly out of downtown, you should check the name of the *colonia* ('neighborhood') and then cross-reference to the street name.

The Zócalo

Mexico revolves around the **Zócalo**, a broad square at the heart of the capital. This stone-paved plaza is the main stage for the nation's political theater, and it is flanked by two of Mexico's most important institutions: the Cathedral and the Presidential Palace. An enormous Mexican flag flies from a massive pole in the Zócalo's center. During the Aztec era, much of this area was the Plaza Mayor ('Great Plaza') of Tenochtitlán, which was surrounded by royal palaces and the most important Aztec temples. The Spanish rebuilt and expanded the plaza on strict rectilinear lines—symbolizing their determination to remake Mexico according to a European system—and the roads radiating out from the square became causeways over which Spanish troops marched to conquer Mexico. The Plaza Mayor became the Plaza de Armas during the colonial

Mexico City's Zócalo and Cathedral, early 1900s, Agustín Casasola

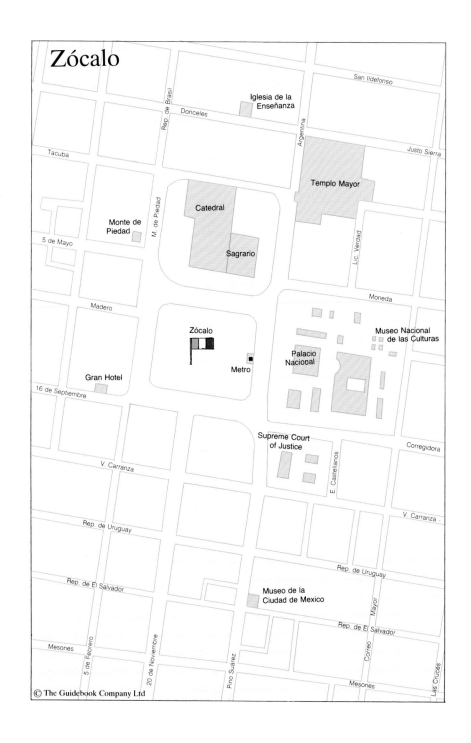

era, and Mexico City's main market was located here until the expanding population made the square too congested. The Zócalo, which is technically named the Plaza de la Constitución, takes its name from the socle, a section of a pedestal, that held up the equestrian statue of Charles IV (1803); this was originally located here but now stands in front of the Museo Nacional de Arte. Today the Zócalo is filled almost daily with official celebrations or with protesters rallying to change (or topple) the government. Every September 15, the plaza is the site of a massive rally to celebrate Mexico's independence. The president appears on the balcony of the National Palace and recites the **Grito de Dolores**, the speech that Miguel Hidalgo used to ignite the insurgency in 1810. The crowd, usually numbering in the hundreds of thousands, responds with roars of *Viva México!*

THE CATHEDRAL AND THE SAGRARIO

The north side of the Zócalo is occupied by the majestic, twin-towered **Cathedral**, the most important in all of Mexico. The original cathedral on this site, begun in 1527, was considered too small and shabby for the colonists' ambitions. They wanted a church 'as big as the one in Seville'. Construction on the present edifice began in the late 16th century, and it was finally finished by 1800. The Cathedral does not exhibit one unified style, either inside or out; classical, baroque, Herrerian, churrigueresque and neo-classical elements are all present in the architecture.

You enter the Cathedral through one of three portals flanked by classical columns. Above each door, framed in solomonic and classical columns, are stone reliefs depicting—from the left—St Thomas doubting, the Assumption of the Virgin Mary (the patroness of the Cathedral) and the Ship of the Church and the Apostles (1687). The upper portions of the façade and towers, including the buttresses, the balustrade that runs the length of the roof, and the unique bell-shaped cupolas on top of the towers were designed by either Damian Ortiz de Castro or Manuel Tolsá, the two great Mexican neo-classical architects.

The Cathedral's interior may come as a shock, because nearly every major arch is now supported by a dense thicket of green scaffolding that obscures most views of the interior's grandeur. The Cathedral suffers from Mexico City's geology and population explosion. Over the last 50 years a greatly increased demand for water has caused the water table to recede, at the same time making the soft clay soil (once the bottom of a lake) sink. The main entrance to the Cathedral is almost three meters lower than the altar at the opposite end. The building's structure was heavily damaged during the 1985 earthquake and is further being weakened by vibrations from a nearby subway line. Restoration experts predicted that the building would collapse within ten years unless something drastic was done immediately—hence the scaffolding. The current plan calls not for the subsidence to stop—thought to be impossible—but for the various parts of the Cathedral to be brought level to each other so that the whole construction sinks at the same rate.

The rectangular interior of the cathedral is divided into five naves: one central, two processional and two that hold the chapels. Your access to all the sights may be blocked if there is a service under way. Sixteen enormous fluted columns divide the central nave from the processionals. Closest to the main entrance, the central nave is occupied by the Choir and the **Altar del Perdón**, which faces the portals. Both were severely damaged in a 1967 fire and what you see is a more-or-less complete reconstruction. The Altar del Perdón (17th century) was so named because it was where prisoners condemned by the Inquisition went to be reconciled with the Church before their imprisonment or execution. The original altar, designed by Jerónimo de Balbas, became the hallmark of the churrigueresque style because it saw the first use of *estípites*, the architectural element that replaced columns. The Choir behind the altar contains ornate carved choir-stalls (17th century) and is topped with the embellished pipes of the Cathedral's organ. The roof just beyond the choir is spanned by the dome, which until the 1967 fire was decorated with neo-classical murals. At the far end of the central nave, beyond the onyx main altar, stands the principal chapel, better known as the **Altar de los Reyes** (1718–25). Also designed by Jerónimo de Balbas, this is one of the masterpieces of the churrigueresque. Deep gilt carvings curve around the back wall and four tall, semi-detached *estípites* hold statues of saints and cherubim. More sculptures of angels peer down from the top of the almost impossibly ornate carvings. In the center, two paintings by Juan Rodríguez Juárez depict the *Adoration of the Kings* and the *Assumption of the Virgin*. Chapels dedicated to Divine Providence and Nuestra Señora de Zapopan flank the Altar de los Reyes.

Many of the Cathedral's 14 side chapels are also worth a visit. If you start from the main entrance, the first on the right side is the **Capilla de Nuestra Señora de las Angustias** with a churrigueresque retable containing a painting of the body of Christ after the Crucifixion. Next comes the **Capilla del Santo Cristo Señor de Veneno**, which houses a black crucifix on the left wall, a baroque portal to the Sagrario next door in the center and a unique gold retable to the right. The following **Capilla de la Inmaculada Concepción** contains a famous painting of St Christopher by Simon Pereyns and 17th-century retables. After two less interesting neo-classical chapels and the closed eastern portal, you come to the **Capilla de San Pedro**, which is decorated with three baroque retables and holds the remains of Juan de Zumárraga, Mexico's first archbishop. The last chapel on this side is the **Capilla de las Reliquias**, housing a piece of the true cross, bones of Santa Hilaria and San Teofilo and three baroque retables. The central retable contains small paintings depicting the martyrdoms of various saints. The next doorway, to the sacristy, was designed in the austere style of Juan de Herrera, who built the Escorial Palace in Spain. Passing the Altar del los Reyes, the first chapel on the opposite wall is the **Capilla de San Felipe de Jesús**. San Felipe, the first Mexican saint, was a missionary in distant Japan during the 16th century and was crucified there with many of his brethren. The chapel's sculpture of the saint, carved shortly after his death, is particularly fine. The urn housing the ashes of Agustín de Iturbide, briefly Mexico's emperor during the 1820s, is also kept here. The next two chapels, both neo-classical, are less interesting. Between them, next to the western portal, is a stairway leading down to the **crypt**, where many of Mexico's archbishops are buried.

Returning to the line of chapels, next you come to the **Capilla de Nuestra Señora de Soledad** with two baroque retables ornamented with solomonic columns. The next chapel, the **Capilla de San José**, contains a churrigueresque retable decorated with a multitude of sculptures growing from the *estipites*. A 16th-century sculpture here, called **El Señor de Cacao**, was paid for with cacao beans during those early colonial days when these were the currency. The following **Capilla de los Santos Cosme y Damian** houses a mid-17th-century baroque retable and a crucifix of Santo Cristo de la Salud. Next to the entrance, the **Capilla de los Santos Ángeles y árcangeles** has three very elaborate baroque retables.

Outside the Cathedral, the monument (1878) about 15 meters (49 feet) west of the main entrance commemorates the German engineer, Enrico Martinez (born Heinrich Martin), who began the massive, centuries-long project of draining the Valley of Mexico to halt the regular flooding of the city. The flooding has stopped, but the project's side-effects—the slow collapse of the Cathedral and the huge slums expanding across the dry lake beds, for example—have been disastrous for the city and its residents.

Immediately to the east of the Cathedral stands the **Sagrario Metropolitano** (18th century), which houses the baptismal font and the church registry for the diocese. The interior seems to be permanently closed for repairs. The south and east façades of the Sagrario are elaborate churrigueresque concoctions made from red and white stone. The south portal is flanked by four *estípites* with inter-*estípites* between them, and the entire stonework is covered with sculptures of saints and animal reliefs. The east portal is less ambitious and harder to see, because the yard in front of it is used to store construction materials for the Cathedral renovation. The Sagrario is built on a Latin-cross shaped plan, and the interior was designed in the neo-classical style with nine altars and a large gilt baptismal font on the left.

The Palacio Nacional

The Palacio Nacional occupies a four-square-block area along the east side of the Zócalo. Motecuhzoma II's palace originally stood here, and after the Conquest it became the property of the Cortés family. The colonial government bought the site in

1562 and converted the building into the Royal Palace, the official seat of the viceroys. The palace has undergone many remodellings over the centuries, most recently in the 1920s, when the third story was added. There are three entrances to the palace: the northernmost communicates with the offices of the Secretaría de Hacienda (Treasury) and is generally closed to tourists; the southern portal is the entrance to the presidential offices and reception halls, which are definitely off-limits. Every September 16th the president appears on the balcony over the central portal and recites the *Grito de Dolores* to an enormous crowd.

The doorway below opens onto a large patio whose walls contain some of the most famous **Diego Rivera murals,** painted between 1929 and 1935. The murals begin in the stairwell to the left of the entry. The central portion illustrates the history of Mexico from the Conquest to the Revolution and teems with portraits of historical figures and caricatures of conquistadors, industrialists and American imperialists. The right hand panel depicts the idyllic Aztec past: the bearded figure of a white man represents Quetzalcoatl, the legendary Toltec king who became an Aztec god. The opposite panel predicts Mexico's future: workers' and peasants' struggles against the evils of capitalism, the whole presided over by a deified 'Carlos' Marx.

You find more Rivera murals along the north wall of the patio's second-story arcade. The first depicts the riches of 'The Great Tenochtitlán'. The female figure in the foreground is artist Frida Kahlo, decorated with the tattooed legs of an Indian prostitute. The next paintings illustrate aspects of Aztec life, including art, ritual and agriculture. The Totonac city of El Tajín is also reconstructed. The last mural shows the cruelty of the conquistadors and includes a portrait of Columbus as a syphilitic fool.

Turn the corner and you come to the **Recinto Parlamentario**, an exhibit

(opposite) The Mexican flag and the National Palace on the Zócalo; (above) Sagrario Metropolitano's churrigueresque façade

containing copies of the 1857 constitution and portraits of the signers. The meeting hall behind is a reproduction of the old chamber of deputies. The northern patio of the palace houses a **Benito Juárez museum** that appears to be under permanent renovation. Along Calle Corregidora at the south side of the building you can see the remains of the old system of canals that was the principle supply route for the Aztec and early colonial city.

THE SOUTH AND EAST SIDES OF THE ZÓCALO

Two buildings housing the **offices of the city government** (the Departamento del Distrito Federal) occupy the south side of the Zócalo. The one nearest the Palacio Nacional is a 1940s construction built on the site of the colonial Portal de Flores, originally a flower market. The building to the west was built as the seat of Mexico's council in 1527 and ever since has held government offices. It has been frequently renovated over the centuries. The portal at street level is decorated with tile-work shields commemorating Columbus, Cortés, the founding of Mexico City and so on. Just across the street and a few steps west down Av 16 de Septiembre, you come to the **Gran Hotel de la Ciudad de Mexico** (1895–98). Originally built as a department store, this building's atrium is one of Mexico's finest examples of art nouveau, with a huge stained-glass elevator and other period elevators.

Returning to the Zócalo, the west side of the square is flanked by the **Portal de Mercaderes**, which has been a shopping center since 1524. Cloth, fruit, herbs, toys and hats have all been sold here, but now it is devoted to jewelry stores (one good hat store, Sombreros Tardán, remains). One block further on, at the northwest corner of the Zócalo, stands the **Nacional Monte de Piedad**, the main offices of a federal public-welfare organization that is best known for its chain of pawn shops found throughout Mexico. Motecuhzoma II's Axayacatl Palace, also known as his 'old houses', stood at this spot, and Cortés tore them down to build an enormous fort-like palace spreading over at least four city blocks. Cortés' palace was gradually whittled down over the years, and in 1836 the government bought the remaining building from one of his descendants. Freelance money-lenders linger at the door looking for easy marks trying to get a good price for their family heirlooms. Inside are long lines of people waiting to sell possessions to the official pawnbrokers; after every holiday the queues extend out the door and around the block. Unredeemed articles may be bought at the auction hall or in one of the many rooms where jewelry, furniture, antiques, computers, books, paintings, cameras and medical instruments are sold for a fixed price. It is fun to browse, but bargains are hard to find. The building also contains a small **museum** on the Monte Piedad's history.

North of the Zócalo

TEMPLO MAYOR

Half a block north from the Zócalo, modern Mexico's hub, stands the center of the Aztec universe. Here, just below street level, are the remains of the **Templo Mayor** ('Great Temple'), built on the exact spot that the Aztecs saw the eagle seated on the nopal cactus in the 14th century. At that time, the site was a swampy island in the middle of a huge lake, and the god Huitzilopochtli decreed that a temple be built in his honor here. Around it they planned a walled sacred precinct with gates in four directions, leading out to the four residential neighborhoods. Beyond these lay the enemy states they were determined to conquer and from which they intended to demand tribute in honor of their god. The design of the Templo Mayor and the surrounding sacred precinct faithfully reproduced the Aztecs' view of the universe and their place at its center.

Archeologists were not able to excavate the temple's earliest foundations, because they lie below the water table, but they believe that the structure's basic form was planned from the outset. The temple faces west and is divided into two, with two staircases and two shrines on top. The south temple was dedicated to Huitzilopochtli; a sacrificial stone called a *tehcatl* was found in front of his shrine. The north temple was devoted to the rain god Tláloc; in front stood a painted *chac mool*, a reclining figure that may have been an intercessor with the gods. According to the Spaniards, both shrines had elaborately carved wooden lintels, murals covering the interior walls and large statues of the respective gods, but neither sculpture has been found; they were probably destroyed by Cortés and his men. The duality of Huitzilopochtli and Tláloc represented the two highest Aztec values: water for abundance and fertility, and war to gain tribute and sacrificial victims. The temple's identification with these gods is strengthened by placing them on top of twin pyramids that represent the sacred mountains central to their myths. The north pyramid symbolizes Tonacatepetl, the 'Hill of Sustenance', a volcano in the state of Puebla where the cult of Tláloc is based. Huitzilopochtli's pyramid represents Coatepec, a hill near Tula where the god defeated his sister Coyolxauhqui and his 400 brothers. An amazing circular stone relief showing Coyolxauhqui's broken corpse was found at the foot of his pyramid, at the base of the hill.

The Aztecs also used the design of the Templo Mayor to illustrate their cosmology. The platform on which the temple rests is surrounded by serpents, representing the terrestrial level. From here the four world directions radiated outward. The 13 heavens of the Aztecs are symbolized by the tiers of the pyramid. As the priests ascended from Earth to the Heavens, they passed through regions of the moon and

On The Plaza

There are city parks and squares in other countries, but in none do they play the same intimate and important part in the national domestic life that they do in Mexico. To one accustomed to associate the 'breathing spaces' with red-nosed tramps and collarless, unemployed men dejectedly reading wilted newspapers on shabby benches, it would be impossible to give an idea of what the plaza means to the people of Mexico—or how it is used by them. It strikes me always as a kind of open-air drawing-room, not only, as are our own public squares, free to all, but, unlike them, frequented by all. It is not easy to imagine one's acquaintances in the United States putting on their best clothes for the purpose of strolling around and around the public square of even one of the smaller cities, to the efforts of a brass band, however good; but in Mexico one's acquaintances take an indescribable amount of innocent pleasure in doing just this on three evenings a week with a simplicity—a democracy—that is a strange contradiction in a people who have inherited so much punctilio—such pride of position, they do it together with all the servants and laborers in town. In the smaller places the men at these concerts promenade in one direction, while the women, and the women accompanied by men, revolve in the other; a convenient arrangement that permits the men to apperceive the charms of the women, and the women to apperceive the charms of the men without effort or boldness on the part of either. And everyone socially is so at ease! There is among the rich and well dressed not the slightest trace of that 'certain condescension' observable, I feel sure, when the duke and duchess graciously pair off with the housekeeper and butler, and among the lower classes—the maid and men servants, the stone-masons and carpenters, the cargadores, the clerks, the small shopkeepers—there is neither the aggressive sense of an equality that does not exist nor a suggestion of servility. The sons of, say, the governor of the state, and their companions, will stroll away the evening between two groups of sandaled Indians with blankets on their shoulders—his daughters in the midst of a phalanx of laundresses and cooks; the proximity being carried off with an engaging naturalness, an apparent unawareness of difference on the part of everyone that is the

Lowering the flag in the Zócalo

perfection of good manners. When such contacts happen with us it is invariably an experiment, never a matter of course. Our upper classes self-consciously regard themselves as doing something rather quaint—experiencing a new sensation, while the lower classes eye them with mixed emotions I have never been able satisfactorily to analyze.

But the serenatas are the least of it. The plaza is in constant use from morning until late at night. Ladies stop there on their way home from church, 'dar una vuelta' (to take a turn), as they call it, and to see and be seen; gentlemen frequently interrupt the labors of the day by going there to meditate over a cigar; schoolboys find in it a shady, secluded bench and use it as a study; nurse maids use it as a nursery; children use its broad, outside walks as a playground; tired workmen use it as a place of rest. By eleven o'clock at night the whole town will, at various hours, have passed through it, strolled in it, played, sat, rested, talked, or thought in it. It is the place to go when in doubt as to what to do with oneself—the place to investigate, when in doubt as to where to find some one. The plaza is a kind of social clearing house—a resource—a solution. I know of nothing quite like it, and nothing as fertile in the possibilities of innocent diversion. Except during a downpour of rain, the plaza never disappoints.

Charles Macomb Flandrau, Viva Mexico!, 1908

clouds, stars, the sun and so on, until they reached the realm of the gods and, finally, the ultimate level, Omeyocan, the place of duality at the twin shrines. The nine levels of the underworld lay beneath the pyramid, terminating at Mictlan, the land of the dead. Thus the Templo Mayor was not only the center of the terrestrial world, it was also the entrance to both the heavens and the underworld—the literal center of the Aztec universe.

The first-time visitor to the Templo Mayor will find nothing as clear-cut as the above description; at first glance, the site looks like a hodgepodge of assorted architectural and sculptural elements. The excavation of the temple began in 1978, after Electric Light Company employees discovered the Coyolxauhqui stone at the corner of Guatemala and Argentina streets. Archeologists guessed that the Templo Mayor of the conquistadors' accounts lay here and decided to raze an entire city block of 18th- and 19th-century buildings to excavate the site. They found that the Spaniards had lopped off the top two-thirds of the temple and appropriated the stones to build their churches and palaces. What was left were the remains of not one temple but seven, one built on top of another during regular expansions. Only some stone flooring of the seventh and final stage remains, because it was the one most destroyed by the Spaniards. The best preserved is the second stage, on top of which the *tehcatl* and the painted *chac mool* are found. To the north of the temple stood three small temples and the Precinct of the Eagle Warriors, which have also been excavated.

The **entrance** to the Templo Mayor is through a colonial building (bookstore is worth visiting) just to the south of the ruins. You perambulate the ruins on a metal walkway with faded explanatory plaques every few meters. The most elevated point of the ruins is the temple in stage II with the above-mentioned *chac mool* and *tehcatl* (dated AD 1390) under a metal roof. All that is left of stage III are a set of stairs, against which lean a few stone sculptures known as 'standard-bearers' that may represent some of the 400 mythic brothers slain by Huitzilopochtli. You can clearly see the division of the stairs that led up to the separate shrines of the gods. A brick-lined sewer built by Porfirio Díaz's son in 1900 cuts through Huitzilopochtli's pyramid. Main points of attraction in stage IV are large ceramic braziers and the serpent heads on each side that still bear traces of red, blue and yellow pigment. Stage IVB was an enlargement of the western façade and included undulating serpent sculptures (symbolizing the terrestrial world) and an altar in the shape of a frog. The Coyolxauhqui stone may date from this era, because it was found at the base of the outer stage IVB steps. The Precinct of the Eagle Warriors and the three small temples, one of which is called the **Tzompantli** ('skull rack') due to the rows of human skulls along the sides, were the main constructions of stage VI. All that remains of stage VII is some ornate flooring.

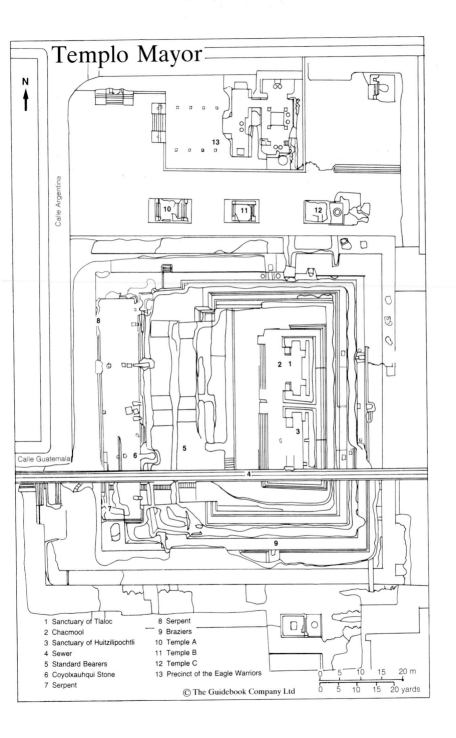

Templo Mayor

N ↑

Calle Argentina

Calle Guatemala

13

10 11 12

8

2 1

3

6 5

4

7

9

1 Sanctuary of Tlaloc	8 Serpent
2 Chacmool	9 Braziers
3 Sanctuary of Huitzilipochtli	10 Temple A
4 Sewer	11 Temple B
5 Standard Bearers	12 Temple C
6 Coyolxauhqui Stone	13 Precinct of the Eagle Warriors
7 Serpent	

© The Guidebook Company Ltd

0   5   10   15   20 m
0   5   10   15   20 yards

The walkway ends at the entrance to the **Templo Mayor Museum** (entrance included in ticket), one of the best designed in Mexico, just to the east of the ruins. All the artefacts here were found during the Templo Mayor excavation, many in the more than 100 offering caches which contained over 6,000 objects buried in the temple by the Aztecs during construction. The first exhibit is a huge diorama of the sacred precinct of Tenochtitlán just before the Conquest. Also here is the incredible, gruesome **Coyolxauhqui stone** (better viewed from the second story); if you look closely you can see traces of blue, ochre, red and black pigments. Coyolxauhqui is shown dismembered and beheaded after her defeat at the hands of her brother and her fall from the Coatepec hill. Her death symbolized the sun's daily victory over night, personified by herself, the moon, and her 400 brothers representing the stars. The exhibits then ascend to excellent displays (all explanations in Spanish) on Aztec beliefs about death and sacrifice and on their system of tribute from vassal states. Many of the objects found in the caches were from vassal states as far away as Veracruz, on the Gulf coast, and Guerrero and Oaxaca along the Pacific. These included shell, jade, stone, obsidian and gold, as well as many plant and animal remains, many from the sea. The top floor contains lifesize eagle warrior ceramic sculptures from the Precinct of the Eagle Warrior and images of Tláloc found beneath his temple. The exhibits descend to displays on the incredible variety of flora and fauna found in the offerings and their religious and economic significance. Next comes a description of the lake system's agriculture and a diorama of the *chinampa* system of cultivation that provided most of the produce for the Aztecs. The museum ends with an exhibit of objects from the Conquest and early colonial eras.

CALLE MONEDA

If you head south after exiting the Templo Mayor, a half-block walk will take you to Calle Moneda flanking the north side of the Palacio Nacional. Immediately east of the palace stands the **Museo Nacional de las Culturas** (entrance is free). This 1731 structure was built to house Mexico's mint, the only one in New Spain until Independence. In the late 19th century, it was transformed into the Anthropology Museum, where Mexico's archeological treasures were held until the new building opened in Chapultepec Park. Today it is a museum that displays objects and the history of cultures from around the world, with many dioramas and reproductions of famous artefacts. Inside the entrance is a 1938 mural by Rufino Tamayo entitled *Revolution*. Across the street, two red-and-gray stone mansions (18th century) on either side of Calle Carmen belonged to the estate of Guerrero, one of the great landowners of colonial Mexico. In the 19th century, the west building became the National Conservatory, while its twin was divided into shops; 20A houses the presses of Mexico's most famous printmaker, José Guadalupe Posada.

Porfiriato decadence by Diego Rivera

East of Calle Carmen, Moneda is renamed Calle Emiliano Zapata. One block further stands the **Academy of San Carlos**, Mexico's most distinguished art school. This building was constructed in the 16th century as a hospital for venereal diseases; the academy took it over shortly after its founding in 1785 and renovated it during the 19th century. Most of the academy's famous art collections are now housed in the Museo de San Carlos (see the Reforma section, page 95) or the Pinacoteca Virreinal next to the Alameda. The interior contains a library, many 19th-century murals and a large numismatic collection. Continuing east, a block's walk takes you to the **Church of the Holy Trinity**, known for its well-preserved churrigueresque façade (1755–83).

FROM THE TEMPLO MAYOR TO THE PLAZA DE SANTO DOMINGO

This tour begins at the intersection of calles Argentina and Justo Sierra at the northeast corner of the Templo Mayor excavations. A few steps west along the north side of Justo Sierra will bring you to the **Iglesia de la Enseñanza** (1778), also known as Nuestra Señora de Piedad. Stepping through a baroque portal with solomonic columns, you enter a small but beautiful church that was built for a convent next door. The interior is decorated with murals and churrigueresque retables along the side walls. The magnificent main altar is surrounded by murals depicting the Ascension, and the altar itself is covered with sculptures rising out of *estipites* that join in a unique rounded top. An iron cage in front of the choir hid the nuns from the public. Across the street and a few doors down stands the **Museo de la Caricatura**, with exhibits of Mexico's most famous editorial cartoonists (you need to have rather a good knowledge of Mexican politics to get the jokes). The museum is housed in the 18th-century building of the College of Christ, a Jesuit school with a fine baroque façade.

Returning to the corner of Argentina and Justo Sierra, the **Librería Porrúa** here is one of the most famous publishers and (Spanish-only) bookstores in Latin America. Immediately east of Porrúa stands the entrance to the Simon Bolívar Amphitheater, part of the **Colegio de San Ildefonso**, where many of the great 20th-century muralists painted their earliest works. You may enter the college either through the amphitheater or via an entry at 43 Calle San Ildefonso on the next block north. The Colegio de San Ildefonso was founded by Jesuits in the 16th century and became one of Mexico's most important schools. The present building dates mostly from a 1712–40 renovation; the Calle San Ildefonso façade and baroque entrances are particularly imposing. In 1867, the building became the National Preparatory School, an élite high school attached to Mexico's national university; in 1978 it was con-verted into a cultural center. The building is divided into two patios, east and west. Immediately after the Revolution, José Vasconcelos, the university rector, hired a group of young artists to decorate the patio walls with murals. These artists included Diego Rivera, José Clemente Orozco and David Alfaro Siquieros. The work they began here revolutionized 20th-century art. The east patio only contains one much-faded mural by Siquieros in the stairwell. Most of the other murals are along the upper walls of the west patio, including *The Farewell* by Orozco, depicting soldiers leaving for battle, and Rivera's *The Creation*. Unfortunately none of the murals are labelled, and generations of students have carved graffiti along the bottoms of the paintings. The Simón Bolivar Auditorium (1929), just off the west patio, contains more Diego Rivera murals. The east patio is now occupied by the **Cineteca**, which screens Mexican and foreign films in a theater next to the entrance, and has a good cinema library on the top floor.

A long block-and-a-half walk east on Calle San Ildefonso takes you to the **Templo de Nuestra Señora de Loreto** opposite a small plaza. This church was initiated in the 16th century, but most of the construction dates from the early 19th century, when the neo-classical façade and interior were completed. The floor plan is unique, with four semi-circular chapels off the circular transept. One block north on Calle Rodríguez Puebla stands the **Mercado Abelardo L Rodríguez** (1938), whose interior is decorated with murals by Pablo O'Higgins and the American sculptor Isamu Nog-uchi, among others. This neighborhood is dense with shops and stalls selling inexpensive clothing.

Return west on San Ildefonso to Calle Argentina. The massive **Secretaría de Educación Pública (SEP) building**, across Argentina and to the right, contains the masterworks of Diego Rivera. Originally built in the 17th century as a convent, the government seized it after ex-cloistering the nuns in 1859. After the Revolution the building became the offices of the education bureaucracy, and it was renovated and expanded. By 1923 José Vasconcelos had become secretary of education, and he commissioned Diego Rivera to paint the walls around the building's twin patios. Over the next five years Rivera covered 1,585 square meters (17,060 square feet) of wall with 124 murals that are now seen as his greatest achievements. The murals along the east patio depict various kinds of work from agricultural to industrial on the ground floor, and the arts on the floor above. The west patio contains portrayals of Mexican fiestas—*The Day of the Dead* is one of his most powerful works—with murals of revolutionary heroes on the upper floors. After years of renovation the building is now open and the murals may be seen in something like their original glory.

Calle San Ildefonso becomes Luis G Obregón after crossing Calle Argentina. After the SEP building, you pass the ex-**Iglesia de la Encarnación** (begun 16th century), now an SEP library, and the **Old Customs Building** (18th century), which houses SEP offices. Both are also undergoing renovation. The street then opens onto the **Plaza de Santo Domingo**, one of the most charming and traditional in Mexico City. During the colonial era this was the city's second most important plaza. Here were an important commercial center and the headquarters of three powerful institutions: Customs, the Inquisition and the Dominican religious order. The **fountain** in the middle bears a seated sculpture of Doña Josefa Ortiz de Domínguez, also known as La Corregidora. In 1810, she warned the insurgent conspirators that royalist forces were about to arrest them, causing them to start the battle for independence. The west side of the plaza is lined with the colonnaded **Portal de Santo Domingo**. This has been a market since the 16th century; originally clothing was sold here. Since the 18th century, the portal has been the center of the public scribe trade. Known as *evangelistas*, these scribes write letters and fill out forms for the illiterate and the uninspired. Few scribes are left, but their places under the arches have been filled by dozens of small, hand-powered printing presses, whose operators solicit business—stationery and wedding announcements—from passers-by. A set of business cards takes about 24 hours.

The surrounding neighborhood is also dominated by the printing trade. The **Templo de Santo Domingo** (18th century), the main church of the Dominican order, occupies the north side of the plaza. The façade is baroque, with a large relief of Santo Domingo over the entry. Inside, two churrigueresque retables flank the nave. On either side of the altar are 11 chapels, the most important of which (third on the left) is dedicated to the Virgin of the Rosary and contains a recent,

An evangelista in the Plaza de Santo Domingo

baroque-style retable. The main altar was designed by the famous neo-classical architect, Manuel Tolsá. A Dominican convent originally stood just west of the church but all except the façade was destroyed in 1859. East of the church across Calle Brasil stands the **Palacio de la Inquisición** (1732–36), the headquarters of the dreaded Holy Office administered by the Dominicans. The Inquisition's mission was to find, punish and convert heretics, mainly Protestants, Jews and anybody with an enemy prone to denunciations. The palace held the Holy Office's courts, prison cells and torture chambers. From these doors issued parades of heretics, who went first to the Cathedral for prayers and then to the Convent of San Diego on the west side of the Alameda for the great *autos da fé*— public whippings and burnings. The Holy Office was abolished in 1820. The palace is now a medical school and contains a small medical museum. About a block west of the Templo de Santo Domingo at 12 Calle B Domínguez is one of Mexico City's finest and oldest restaurants, the **Hostería de Santo Domingo**. It is known for the best *chiles en nogada* (chilli stuffed with rice and ground meat and topped with a walnut sauce), the Mexican national dish; they also serve seasonal specialties like *escamoles* ('ant pupae') and *gusanos de maguey* ('maguey worms').

South of the Zócalo

The severe-looking **Supreme Court of Justice** (1935–41), just south of the Palacio Nacional on Av Pino Suárez, contains four visionary murals by José Clemente Orozco at the top of the main staircase. Entitled The *Social Movement of Work, Justice* (two panels) and *National Riches*, they portray such a violent and corrupt system of justice that immediately after their 1941 unveiling lawyers campaigned to have them removed. A block west on Av V Carranza stands the **Palacio de Hierro** ('Iron Palace'), Mexico City's most famous department store, with multiple floors of upscale clothing and other goods built around an atrium. Right across 20 de Noviembre stands its main competition, the **Liverpool department store**, and the surrounding blocks are filled with stores selling inexpensive shoes and clothing for women and children.

Back to Av Pino Suárez, the **Museo de la Ciudad de México**, two blocks south of the Supreme Court building, is housed in the mansion of the counts of Santiago Calimaya (begun in 1536 and frequently rebuilt). The stones along the base of the façade were supposedly taken from Aztec temples, and the remains of a serpent's head may be seen built into the southeast corner of the building. The elegant main entrance is flanked by columns, and unique cannon-shaped gargoyles jut out from the roof. The interior patio and rooms retain much of the colonial décor and ambiance. The museum contains good exhibitions, with many dioramas and paintings, on the history and cultures of the Valley of Mexico from prehistoric times through the Revolution.

Diagonally across Av Pino Suárez stands the fort-like **Templo y Hospital de Jesús** (begun 1524), which is built on the supposed site of the 8 November 1519 first meeting of Cortés and Motecuhzoma. The hospital, still in operation, was founded by Cortés himself and may have been the first in the New World. The now austere church interior was originally decorated with many opulent retables. The artistic highlight is José Clemente Orozco's black vision of the Apocalypse (1942–44), which decorates

Witches' brew: dried fish in the Mercado de Sonora

the poorly-lit ceiling above the choir. Cortés' bones are buried with little fanfare beside the altar. Passions still run high about the conquistador 500 years after his death; the rediscovery of his bones in 1946 led to a national controversy pitting those who revered him as the founder of modern Mexico against those who reviled him as an arch-villain and genocidal maniac. The **Pino Suárez Metro Station** three blocks south contains the remains, now restored, of a small Aztec pyramid dedicated to Quetzalcoatl.

The adventurous will now want to walk seven blocks east to the enormous **Mercado de la Merced**, just across the broad avenue of Eje 1 Oriente. Set in a run-down neighborhood, this four-block-long building used to be the main wholesale market for the city. Many of the wholesalers have moved to roomier quarters just north of the Iztapalapa neighborhood, but La Merced is still as bustling as ever. Here you can buy an incredible array of fruits, vegetables, meat, fish, housewares, clothing, restaurant supplies, crafts, and so on. During the Day of the Dead celebrations, the vendors construct famously elaborate altars to their ancestors. If this is not enough for you, head two blocks southeast across Av Fray Servando to the **Mercado de Sonora**, also known as the 'Witches' Market'. The vendors here sell toys, candy, herbal medicine and a weird variety of spells and potions—all white magic (I hope).

To return to the Zócalo area, walk four blocks north of the Merced Metro along Eje 1 Oriente to Calle Rep de Uruguay and then head west three blocks until you come to the **Convento de la Merced** (1602–45). All that remains of this once-opulent church/convent complex is the convent's cloister, a courtyard surrounded by two stories of carved baroque colonnades, perhaps the most elaborate in all of Mexico. West of the convent, Calle Uruguay is lined with fabric and notions stores.

The Alameda to the Zócalo

The streets between the Zócalo and the Alameda Park are rich with colonial mansions, churches, museums, banks, restaurants, mid-range to inexpensive hotels and shopping. Most of the sights can be found along the four parallel streets—Calles Tacuba, Cinco de Mayo, Francisco Madero and 16 de Septiembre—which connect the two squares. This tour begins at the southwest corner of the Zócalo at the beginning of Calle 16 de Septiembre.

A two block walk west takes you to Calle Isabela La Católica, with a Sanborn's on the corner. Two blocks to the left (south) stands the **Biblioteca Nacional**, originally built as a church (1541–86, rebuilt 17th century) by the Augustinian order. The baroque façade contains salomonic columns and a square relief of St Augustine over the doorway. The interior was gutted during the 19th century to make way for the library, and you will also notice the significant tilt of the floor due to subsidence. Almost all the books have long ago been moved to the national university (UNAM) campus, but 18 statues of intellectual heroes were left behind, including Homer, Dante, Descartes and Alexander von Humboldt, whose statue also graces the garden outside. Returning to Calle 16 de Septiembre, just to the north you come to the **Casino Español** (1901–03), an ornate edifice containing a Spanish restaurant and the Salón de Reyes ('Salon of Kings') reception hall, filled with mirrors and chandeliers and worth a peek. A half block further north across Calle Francisco I Madero stands the Jesuit-built **Templo de la Profesa** (1720), also known as San Felipe Neri, with a somber baroque façade. The interior contains a neo-classical altar and other décor by the famous architect Manuel Tolsá as well as many paintings.

Our tour now heads west on Calle Francisco I Madero. A few doors past Calle Bolívar, two blocks west, is the **American Bookstore**, Madero 25, perhaps the best English bookstore in the city, with an unparalleled selection of academic books on Mexican anthropology and archeology. In the middle of the same block stands the **Palacio Iturbide** (begun 1779), one of the city's finest baroque palaces and now a branch of Banamex. The building was originally built as a home for a noble family but is named for Mexico's short-lived Emperor Iturbide, who lived here in 1821. For most of the 19th century and up until 1928, it was a luxury hotel. Today Banamex houses excellent temporary exhibitions (free) in the patio. The palace's façade is covered with decoration, including reliefs of mythological subjects, coats-of-arms and two figures of Hercules holding up the higher balcony. The interior courtyard is a copy of the one in the Royal Palace in Palermo, Sicily; the stonework here is also heavily adorned with medallions, gargoyles and the like. The **Templo de San Francisco** (begun 1524), one block west, was once one of the largest and most important convents in the city. An open chapel here was the first church space built specifically for Indian converts in the New World. The entrance is down some steps—a mark of how much the building has sunk over the centuries—and across a courtyard to the Balvanera Chapel, which was built with a fine churrigueresque façade, now pollution-blackened, in the 18th century. The chapel contains a churrigueresque retable holding a sculpture of the church's patron saint. The main church is less interesting; the ornate neo-classical altar is the only jewel; the walls are covered with rather ugly modern murals depicting the life of St Francis. The 16th-century **Casa de los Azulejos** ('House of Tiles') across the street is one of the most unique and famous colonial buildings. In the 18th century, this structure, owned by the counts of Orizaba, was remodelled and decorated with blue tiles in the style of Puebla, but far more beautiful than anything now standing in that nearby city. During the era of Porfirio Díaz, the building housed the Jockey Club, where Mexico City's élite amused themselves at billiards and other entertainments. The Sanborn's restaurant and department store chain now occupies the

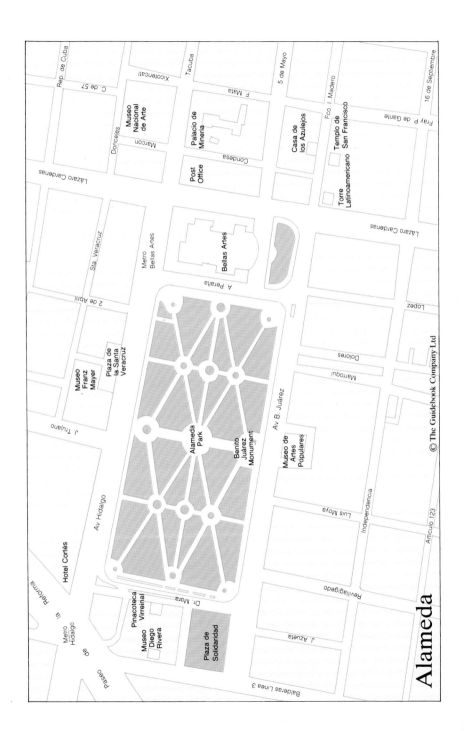

Alameda

interior. There is always a line for the main dining room—traditionally a spot for politicians' power breakfasts—which is located in a beautiful courtyard framed with tall columns and covered with a translucent roof that casts a glow over the scene. The landing of the main staircase is decorated with a mural entitled *Omniscience* by José Clemente Orozco, which frames the entrance to the bathrooms. A wide variety of local crafts are for sale on the second floor.

Diagonally across the street, at the corner of Madero and Eje Central Lázaro Cár-denas stands the 46-story skyscraper, the **Torre Latinoamericana** (1956). In appearance a copy of New York's Empire State Building, the Torre's innovative structural design allowed it to ride out the 1957 and 1985 earthquakes with little damage. Pollution permitting, the observation platform on floors 42–44 has a great view of the surrounding city. You can also visit the Muralto restaurant and bar on the 41st floor and the aquarium—'the highest in the world'—on the 38th. A block to the south, the **Pastelería Ideal**—just east of the intersection of Lázaro Cárdenas and 16 de Septiembre—is the city's most renowned cake and pastry store. The appearance of the Ideal's distinctive white boxes at a dinner party is a sure sign that the host did not stint on dessert.

Calle 5 de Mayo, parallel to and one block north of Calle Madero, has few historical sights but many bookstores and restaurants. The **L'Héritage** restaurant at 10a features Mexican *haute cuisine*, and the **Bar La Opéra** (10) has an excellent lunch menu; it must be visited if only to see its elaborate carved wood interior. Three blocks east is the **Café La Blanca** (40), one of Mexico City's most famous cafeterias; across the street at 39 stands the **Dulcería de Celaya**, the city's premier candy store, selling delicious traditional sweets in an art nouveau interior.

Returning to Eje Central Lázaro Cárdenas, just north of the stern art deco **Banco de Mexico** building on the corner of Calle 5 de Mayo is the ornate **Post Office** (1902–07). This was built under orders of Porfirio Díaz to show the cutting edge of technology—the plan called for electric lights, elevators and telephones—and to display the architect's skills. The façade, which vaguely resembles a Venetian palace, contains details in almost every European architectural style in fashion in 1900. It is worth a trip to buy stamps here; the surly clerks sit behind elaborate iron bars and the postcard vendors at the door have the best selection in the city.

Next door on Calle Tacuba stands the **Palacio de Minería** (1797–1813), until 1860 the government school of mines, which was the masterwork of the neo-classical architect, Manuel Tolsá. The stern, rationalistic design was intended to put to rest the extravagances of the churrigueresque. Schools and government offices were housed here for many years, but since a major renovation in the 1970s the building is now used for special events and exhibitions. Just inside the main entrance, visitors may see a few of the larger meteorites that have fallen on Mexico over the last century.

City of Cities

Paco Ignacio Taibo II is one of the world's most widely read mystery writers. Born in Spain in 1949, he moved to Mexico as a youth and has been a Mexican citizen since 1980. During the 1960s, he was active in the student movement and in film-making. A prolific writer, he has written novels, history books and short story collections, many of which have been bestsellers. He is best known around the world for his terminally lonely, trench-coated detective, Hector Belascoarán Shayne. Hector's profession is the impossible: to find truth and justice in a corrupt, violent and byzantinely complex society. His work takes him across Mexico, but his home—and the real heart of all the mysteries—is Mexico City, where evil and injustice thrive on the blood of innocents. Mr Taibo has generously given us the following tour of his Mexico City:

There are thousands of cities inside Mexico City. Our first tour, the 'frontiers' tour, takes us to the boundaries of the two biggest: the inner city of the middle class, and the outer city of the poor and the factories. The statues of the Indios Verdes, the 'Green Indians', are the northern boundary; beyond lie the industrial wastelands. East, the statue of General Zaragoza is the limit; if you go any further, you are in the huge slums of Ciudad Netzahualcoyotl. To the south, the frontier is the Villa Olimpica, beyond which lies the Tierra Zapatista, the land controlled by the peasant revolutionary Emiliano Zapata during the Revolution. In the west, if you pass the enormous H Steel Company clock, you are in the factory and refinery zone again.

Next we tour the Interior, the Conradian 'Heart of Darkness' of which is the Zócalo. Here is the terminus for all our political demonstrations, where the huge Mexican flag flies in front of the Presidential Palace. You can feel the awful emanations of power. At the nearby Templo Mayor museum—one of the best organized in Mexico—the exhibits put you in touch with the Mexican idea of death and with the city's origins. Then go down into the Metro Zócalo station and experience over-population first hand. The Mexico City Metro is one of the best subways in the world. It is clean in a city that is not clean and safe in a city that is not safe. People feel solidarity here and protect the Metro and their fellow passengers. They will help you not to die.

Another city-within-a-city is Stupid Mexico. This is the shortest tour: simply close the door of your hotel room and watch the Televisa channels all day. This is also the most dangerous; you might not come back.

For a tour of the city of young people, go to one of the rock clubs like Rocko-titlan or Foro Lucc. They are very cheap, urban and peaceful; the cops do not like the music, so they do not bother you. The bands, like Maldita Vecindad and Los Caifanes, are excellent and their songs have great lyrics.

At this point it would be healthy to climb up to Chapultepec Castle and have the same view over the city as the Emperor Maximilian. It is good to look down on the city for once, instead of always looking up. The views of the park and of the beginning of the Paseo de la Reforma are the best in the city.

Another city is the City of Markets. Head north of the Zócalo to where the streets are all closed, where you can hardly walk because of all the stalls and where everybody is selling something. But who has the money to buy? And if everybody is selling, who is producing all this stuff? This tour is the best way to discover that modern economics does not make sense.

Our last tour is to the City of Smog. Go to the top of the Torre Latinoameri-cana on a very smoggy day when you can not see anything but the gray-green cloud. Now try to discover what is behind the cloud. Is anybody down there? You used to be able to commit suicide from here, but not anymore since they put up the nets. Every big city needs a place to jump, but it should be somewhere where you can do it without killing anyone.

Plaza Rio de Janeiro

Cantina scene, early 1900s, Enrique Díaz

Across Calle Tacuba, a little plaza holds the heroic bronze **Equestrian Statue of Charles IV** (1803), also designed by Tolsá. Nicknamed **El Caballito** ('The Little Horse') by locals, this sculpture of the King of Spain presided over the center of the Zócalo for two decades and then was shunted to lesser positions around the city until arriving at this spot in 1981. There are rumors that Tolsá copied his design from a sculpture of Louis XIV of France. **El Caballito** stands in front of the **Antiguo Palacio de Comunicaciones** (1904–11), now the **Museo Nacional de Arte**. This homage to Tolsá and his fellow neo-classicists was built to house the Secretariat of Communications under Porfirio Díaz and has been home to the art museum since 1982. The collection is made up of Mexican painting and sculpture since the pre-Hispanic era, being particularly strong on the 19th and early 20th centuries. Among the highlights are a room devoted to the 19th-century landscapes of the Valley of Mexico by José María Velasco, depicting a beautiful pre-industrial setting. It is a relief to see how, in the early 20th century, Mexican painters stopped producing slavish copies of European academic styles and forged their own distinctly Mexican art. A block and a half east of the museum you come to the **Café Tacuba** (Calle Tacuba 28), founded in 1912 and one of the most popular traditional restaurants. The interior is lined with tiles and copies of famous colonial portraits. In the back, a triptych mural depicts the history of chocolate in colonial Mexico, from the apocryphal invention of *mole* in

Puebla's Santa Rosa convent through the aristocracy sipping their chocolate drink and on to middle-class ladies snacking on chocolate candies. In late October, this is a good place to buy your sweet **Pan de los Muertos** ('Bread of the Dead').

Back to Lázaro Cárdenas. North of Calle Tacuba, this broad avenue becomes the city's popular entertainment center, now somewhat dimmed by earthquakes and urban renewal. Here you will find movie theaters, record stores, dubious bars, burlesque clubs and the **Teatro Blanquita** with family-oriented variety shows. **Calle Donceles**, a block north of Tacuba, is lined with used bookstores four blocks to the east, many with English-language sections. Three streets north and three blocks east, on Calle Rep de Perú, stands the **Arena Coliseo**, one of Mexico City's most illustrious arenas for boxing and professional wrestling. Continuing north on Lázaro Cárdenas, a half block beyond Perú (opposite the **Teatro Garibaldi** burlesque theater), you come to the celebrated **Plaza Garibaldi**, where the spirit of Mexican traditional music is kept alive every evening. At one end of the plaza stands the **Statue of Pedro Infante**, idol of song and screen, who died tragically in a 1957 plane crash. Across the plaza is the **Statue of the Mariachi**, representing the Guadalajara-style musicians whose songs have become Mexico's traditional music. Every evening the plaza swarms with *mariachis* wearing their Jalisco cowboy outfits of boots, tight pants with two rows of silver buttons along the legs, short jackets, bow-ties and broad embroidered hats. They practice, serenade tourists and solicit work on Lázaro Cárdenas from any passers-by who need entertainment for a party. The plaza is surrounded by restaurants, nightclubs and bars, some sedate, others wild, generally filled with music and merry-makers (watch out for pickpockets and thieves). At the northeast end of the plaza is one of the city's cleanest *pulquerías*, **La Hermosa Hortencia**, where you may try this milky, refreshing, somewhat foul-smelling but surprisingly effective drink that was the favorite alcoholic beverage of the Aztecs. A few doors west is the entrance to the **Mercado San Camilito**, which is filled with dozens of snack bars serving Jalisco-style roast meats, goat, seafood and *pozole* (hominy stew with meat), attracting hungry drinkers and *mariachis* late into the night. Just east of the plaza is the smaller **Plaza Santa Cecilia**, home to **Garibaldy's** [sic], a very loud disco, and the family-oriented **Teatro Santa Cecilia**, which bills itself as the 'Cathedral of Folkloric Music and Dance in Mexico'.

Lázaro Cárdenas then runs into the Paseo de la Reforma at a large traffic circle. On Sundays, the streets to the east of the circle are closed to traffic and filled with vendors selling antiques, books and a million other wares as an extension of the Lagunilla Market two blocks east. This used to be known as the 'Thieves' Market', where you could purchase articles as diverse as old dueling pistols and complete sets of *Mad Magazine*. In recent years, vendors of T-shirts and electronics goods have invaded this terrain, but browsing remains an adventure (beware of pickpockets). All

Directors' Revenge

In addition to their machismo, Mexicans have a highly developed capacity for vengeance. My assistant on Subida al cielo *once told me a story about the time he went hunting on Sunday with a few friends. They'd just stopped for lunch when they found themselves surrounded by armed men on horseback who took away their boots and rifles. One man in the group was a friend of an important official who lived nearby, and when they went to protest, the official asked them to describe their attackers as closely as they could.*

'And now,' he added, once the description was complete, 'allow me to invite you for a drink next Sunday.'

When they returned the following week, their host served them coffee and liqueurs, then asked them to come into the next room, where, to their amazement, they found their boots and rifles. When they asked who their attackers had been and if they could see them, the official only smiled and told them the case was closed. Indeed, the aggressors were never seen again—by anyone—just as thousands of people simply 'vanish' each year in Latin America. The League of the Rights of Man and Amnesty International do their best, but the disappearances continue.

Interestingly enough, in Mexico a murderer is designated by the number of lives he 'owes'. People say he owes so many lives; and when the police get their hands on someone who owes a lot of them, they don't bother with formalities. I remember an incident that occurred while we were making La Mort en ce jardin *near Catemaco Lake. The local police chief, who'd waged a vigorous campaign to rid the area of outlaws, came by one day and casually invited the French actor George Marchal, who had a passion for hunting, to accompany him on a manhunt for a well-known killer. Horrified, Marchal refused. But several hours later, when the police passed again, the chief stopped to inform us that the business had now been taken care of and that we had nothing more to fear.*

There is a peculiarly intimate relationship between Mexicans and their guns. One day I saw the director Chano Urueta on the set directing a scene with a Colt .45 in his belt.

'You never know what might happen,' he replied casually, when I asked him why he needed a gun in the studio.

On another occasion, when the union demanded that the music for Ensayo de un crimen (The Criminal Life of Archibaldo de la Cruz) be taped, thirty musicians arrived at the studio one very hot day, and when they took off their jackets, fully three quarters of them were wearing guns in shoulder holsters.

The writer Alfonso Reyes told me about the time, in the early 1920s, that he went to see Vasconcelos, then the secretary of public education, for a meeting about Mexican traditions.

'Except for you and me,' Reyes told him, 'everyone here seems to be wearing a gun!'

'Speak for yourself,' Vasconcelos replied calmly, opening his jacket to reveal a Colt .45.

continues

Young revolutionary soldier, Agustín Casasola

This 'gun cult' in Mexico has innumerable adherents, including the great Diego Rivera, whom I remember taking out his pistol one day and idly sniping at passing trucks. There was also the director Emilio 'Indio' Fernández, who made María Candelaria and La perla, and who wound up in prison because of his addiction to the Colt .45. It seems that when he returned from the Cannes Festival, where one of his films had won the prize for best cinematography, he agreed to see some reporters in his villa in Mexico City. As they sat around talking about the ceremony, Fernández suddenly began insisting that instead of the cinematography award, it had really been the prize for best direction. When the newspapermen protested, Fernández leapt to his feet and shouted he'd show them the papers to prove it. The minute he left the room, one of the reporters suspected he'd gone to get not the papers, but a revolver—and all of them took to their heels just as Fernández began firing from a second-story window. (One was even wounded in the chest.)

The best story, however, was told me by the painter Siqueiros. It occurred toward the end of the Mexican Revolution when two officers, old friends who'd been students together at the military academy but who'd fought on opposing sides, discovered that one of them was a prisoner and was to be shot by the other. (Only officers were executed; ordinary soldiers were pardoned if they agreed to shout 'Viva' followed by the name of the winning general.) In the evening, the officer let his prisoner out of his cell so that they could have a drink together. The two men embraced, touched glasses, and burst into tears. They spent the evening reminiscing about old times and weeping over the pitiless circumstances that had appointed one to be the other's executioner.

'Whoever could have imagined that one day I'd have to shoot you?' one said.

'You must do your duty,' replied the other. 'There's nothing to be done about it.'

Overcome by the hideous irony of their situation, they became quite drunk.

'Listen my friend,' the prisoner said at last. 'Perhaps you might grant me a last wish? I want you, and only you, to be my executioner.'

Still seated at the table, his eyes full of tears, the victorious officer nodded, pulled out his gun, and shot him on the spot.

Luis Buñuel, My Last Sigh, 1981, trans Abigail Israel

the surrounding streets have also been converted into open markets, many selling cheap clothing and shoes. Dedicated explorers may want to continue their shopping in the legendary **Barrio de Tepito**, eight blocks east on Av Héroe de Granaditas (Eje 1 Norte) and then a block north on Calle Florida. For centuries until the 1985 earthquake, Tepito was Mexico City's most famous tough neighborhood, breeding ground for gangsters, entertainers and famous boxers like Kid Azteca. Many of the barrio's old buildings were destroyed during the earthquake; afterward the government encouraged residents to move to new housing on the outskirts of the city, sapping Tepito of its density and dynamism. Although to locals the area is a shadow of its former self, visitors may still be impressed by the volume of activity on the streets. The main avenues are lined with wholesale shoe stores, whose deliverymen rush frantically about with huge stacks of boxes. The center of Tepito is clogged with a vast market best known for its low-priced electronic goods (protected until recently by tariffs). As you penetrate deeper, you will come across halls where vendors sell used clothing by weight and junk, like dolls' heads and knobs from old radios, scavenged from the street. At night, Tepito reverts to its old habits of prostitution and thuggery.

Around the Alameda

In 1592, Don Luis de Velasco, the *Virrey* ('viceroy'), ordered the construction of an *alameda*, a tree-lined walk, to 'ornament the city and give recreation to its citizens'. By the latter, the *Virrey* meant the colonial élite, because the park was walled and the ragged, the dirty and all Indians were forbidden entry through the gates (*their* playground was the Zócalo's messy marketplace). It became the favorite promenade of rich aristocrats who loved to display their wealth; dressed in their finest, they came in elegant carriages surrounded by retinues of servants. The park was also a breeding ground for patrician flirtations, which occasionally led to duels between jealous gallants. Today the **Alameda Park**, seven blocks east of the Zócalo, still conforms to the *Virrey's* orders, although the rich have long since disappeared into exclusive suburbs. Every day it is crowded with families, courting couples, balloon vendors, snake-oil salesman, dealers of revolutionary books, and so on. The Alameda is also filled with fountains and sculptures, mostly with a mythological theme. On the south side of the park, the white-Carrara-marble **Monument to Benito Juárez**, also known as the Juárez Hemicycle, was built for Porfirio Díaz's 1911 Centennial of the Revolution celebration; Juárez, famous for his aversion to pomp, most certainly would have disapproved (perhaps it was a form of revenge by his old rival). On weekends there are concerts by top Mexican entertainers in the park's west end.

At the eastern end of the park stands the wedding-cake-like edifice of the **Palacio de Bellas Artes** (1904–1934). Porfirio Díaz commissioned Bellas Artes (as it is familiarly known) to be a theater that would rival the Paris Opera in splendor. The white marble façade is decorated with neo-classical details depicting serpents, eagles and other Mexican motifs and sculptural groupings with themes like 'Apollo and the Muses'. Construction was stopped by the Revolution in 1916, with only the exterior completed; in 1930 work began again, and the interior was completed in the art deco style. The theater in Bellas Artes is now used for concerts and weekly Ballet Folklórica dance performances. The first floor contains temporary exhibition spaces, while the second and third floors have some of the most famous murals by Orozco (*Catharsis*), Rivera (*Universal Man and the Machine*—a reproduction of the Rockefeller Center mural that was destroyed in a controversy over its political imagery, *Dictatorship*, *The Dance of Huichilobos* and *Folkloric and Touristic Mexico*), Siquieros (*Victims of War and Victims of Fascism*) and Rufino Tamayo (*Birth of Our Nationality*). Bellas Artes also houses a very good bookstore.

Calle Dolores, which heads south from the east end of the Alameda, contains Mexico City's small **Chinatown**. The **San Juan Artisan's Market**, four blocks south of the Alameda on Dolores, has two floors of shops selling textiles, jewelry, leather and ceramics to the tourist trade. Prices here are relatively high and the goods are not the most authentic in town. The air is suffused with the smell of coffee from the nearby wholesale coffee grinders. If you want to see a traditional neighborhood market, the **Mercado San Juan** just across the little square is one of the best and not nearly as daunting as La Merced.

Returning to the Alameda, the **Museo de Artes y Industrias Populares** (44 Av Juárez), one block west and opposite the Juárez monument, is a large and excellent government crafts store commonly called 'Artes Pops'. Unfortunately it recently began what looks like being a years-long renovation. It is housed in the ex-church of Corpus Christi (1720–24), with a baroque façade, which was the centerpiece of a much larger convent, now destroyed. A wall inside is covered with a mural by Miguel Covarrubias, the artist and writer, depicting the *Map of Mexican Popular Arts*. The store is filled with inexpensive folk crafts, mainly textiles, toys and holiday decorations, all fashioned by Indian artisans. In October, they have a particularly good Day of the Dead collection and construct a large altar in the front room. Many of the surrounding buildings were heavily damaged in the 1985 earthquake and have yet to be torn down. Another good crafts store, **FONART**, occupies a building a block west of the Alameda on Av Juárez.

The **Plaza de la Solidaridad**, just beyond the southwest corner of the Alameda, was the site of the Hotel del Prado, which collapsed with great loss of life in the 1985 earthquake. A seemingly permanent encampment of left-wing protesters now occupies

the plaza. On the north side stands the **Museo Diego Rivera**, which stages temporary exhibitions. The highlight of this museum is Rivera's huge 1947–48 mural, *Dream of a Sunday Afternoon in the Central Alameda*, which originally decorated the lobby of the Hotel del Prado. The mural shows the park filled with over 120 figures from Mexican history gathered under the broad trees. The front row depicts those who typically would have visited the Alameda in the early part of this century, under the dictatorship of Porfirio Díaz. From left to right, here are the Europeanized élite (one being pickpocketed), sleeping vagrants, vendors, elegant women, a war veteran, foreign tourists, and a policeman expelling an Indian family. Rivera included at least two portraits of himself—as a child on the far right eating bread, and in the center as a schoolboy holding the hand of a womanly Death (her other hand holds the arm of Posada, the famous printmaker). Frida Kahlo stands right behind the pair holding a fruit. The back row gives portraits of Mexican historical figures from 1521 through the Revolution, including, from the left: Cortés, heretics being whipped, Sor Juana, Emperor Iturbide, Juárez, Maximilian, Porfirio Díaz (next to the balloon), Zapata on horseback, Madero and Pancho Villa. The **Pinacoteca Virreinal**, a half block north of the Rivera Museum on the west end of the Alameda, was originally the Convent of San Diego (begun 1594), outside of which stood the main pyre for burning heretics during the Inquisition. The church, which was remodelled along neo-classical lines in the 19th century, houses the great collection of colonial paintings from the Academy of San Carlos. Two hundred and twenty-nine masterpieces of religious art are on display here, as well as copies of pre-Hispanic codices. A 1959 mural by Federico Cantú depicts Indians explaining their beliefs to Fray Bernardo Sahagún, who wrote the best descriptions of their religions that we possess to this day.

The **Hotel Cortés** (85 Av Hidalgo), just across the street from the northwest corner of the Alameda, was built in the 16th century to house Augustinian friars heading out to missionary work in the provinces. After passing through the dark-red-stone baroque façade, you come to a pleasant patio where you can have drinks and rest from the fatigues of tourism. The interior has been heavily remodelled over the centuries. Heading east along Av Hidalgo and the north side of the Alameda, you come to the small **Plaza de la Santa Veracruz** with three fountains in the middle. This square is surrounded on three sides by colonial church buildings that are all tilting drastically in different directions due to ground subsidence. The severely lopsided **Templo de San Juan de Dios** (18th century) on the left has a baroque façade with unique undulating pilasters and a huge scallop over the entrance. The redecorated neo-classical interior contains two marble retables and a fine wood pulpit. Along the north side of the plaza stands the **Museo Franz Mayer**, originally the Hospital of San Juan de Dios (begun 17th century). This large structure, built around two patios, now houses the amazing collection of Mexican colonial fine and applied arts amassed by Franz Mayer, a German-born financier. On the ground floor are exhibitions devoted to furniture, silverware, crystal, wooden sculpture, ceramics and tapestry. On the floor above, you may view watches, European and Mexican paintings and tableware. Religious sculptures made from corn paste are among the many oddities on display. One of the patios houses a café and a good art bookstore with a nearby fountain to soothe the soul. Next door is the smaller **Museo Nacional de la Estampa**, the national print museum, with temporary exhibitions, an introduction to print-making and not enough Posada prints on permanent display. To its right, tilting the opposite way from San Juan de Dios, stands the **Iglesia de la Santa Veracruz**. Begun in 1759, this small church is faced with a churrigueresque façade and even more elaborate churrigueresque carvings around the Av Hidalgo entrance. The interior has been neo-classicized and thus appropriately holds the remains of the champion of that style, Manuel Tolsá.

Reforma and Chapultepec

A muddy road used to connect the Alameda and Chapultepec Hill after the intervening land was drained in the 17th century. The Emperor Maximilian, who placed a very high value on the trappings of office, soon tired of his daily commute to the Palacio Nacional along a route honored only by poor peasants and the unblinking gazes of cattle chewing their cud. In 1864, he decreed the construction of a broad, tree-lined avenue, the Paseo del Emperador, on which his magnificent coach could travel without being spattered by mud. After his capture and execution by Juárez's army, the avenue was renamed Paseo de la Reforma and lined with heroic statues, now pollution-darkened, of politicians and generals who supported the winning side in the Wars of Reform. Today the **Paseo de la Reforma**, commonly called 'Reforma', is choked with traffic (crossing it is an adventure), but the eight-lane-wide avenue still retains enough of its ambience, and trees, to merit its comparison to Paris' Champs Élysées. In the late 19th century, Reforma was the site of a building boom during which many elegant mansions were built along the avenue. Unfortunately, few are left because they have been replaced by corporate headquarters, newspaper offices, expensive hotels, movie theaters and embassies. The current Reforma skyline—boldly jutting mirrored skyscrapers—projects the image of Mexico as a modern economic powerhouse that the current government desperately wants the rest of the world to see.

Av Juárez crosses Reforma from the south end of the Alameda (note the art déco **Old National Lottery Building** at the intersection) and ends at the **Plaza de la Repú-**

(above) *Chapultepec Castle*
(below) *Hideaway mansion in Lomas de Chapultepec*

blica. This plaza is dominated by the **Monument to the Revolution**, a large dome held up by four huge columns, generally regarded as one of Mexico City's ugliest monuments. This black-stone structure was begun in 1910 by Porfirio Díaz as part of a new legislative palace. Construction was stopped by the Revolution, and it was transformed into a brutalist, art deco-style monument in the 1930s. The tops of the columns contain sculptural groups depicting Independence, Reform, Labor Laws and Agricultural Laws. The remains of Pancho Villa and presidents Carranza, Madero, Calles and Cárdenas have been interred in the bases of the columns. Housed in the basement of the monument is the **Museum of the Revolution**, with good audiovisual displays on the chronology of the Revolution. The **Frontón México** on the north side of the square is the nation's premiere arena for *jai alai*. Millions of pesos are gambled there nightly, but unfortunately admission seems to be reserved for the wealthy and connected. Two blocks north on Calle Arizpe stands the **Museo de San Carlos** in an elegant colonial mansion (rebuilt 1795) that contains the European painting collection of the Academy of San Carlos, the first art academy in the New World. On display are works by Goya, Zurbarán, Rubens and Brueghel. Good temporary exhibitions are also housed here. The Academy's colonial Mexican art collection is housed in the Pinacoteca Virreinal on the west side of the Alameda. Four blocks west of the Museo de San Carlos, at 10 Calle Enrique González Martinez, stands a cathedral-like cast iron building that is now home to the **Museo Universitario del Chopo**, the city's most famous alternative art space. This building was imported from Germany around 1900 and used first as an exhibition hall and later, until 1964, as the natural history museum. Now it houses exhibits of post-modern art with a strong political slant as well as a theater and a free university associated with UNAM.

Returning to Reforma, the first traffic circle contains a **Statue of Christopher Columbus** (1877) surrounded by four smaller statues of Spanish priests and standing on a red marble pedestal. The next traffic circle, at the intersection of Av Insurgentes, contains the **Statue of Cuauhtémoc** (1887), the last Aztec king. Two bronze plaques on the pedestal depict scenes from his life, and the names of other famous Aztec chieftains are also inscribed there. On August 21, the anniversary of Cuauhtémoc's death, Indian groups hold demonstrations here

Imperial opulence, Chapultepec Castle

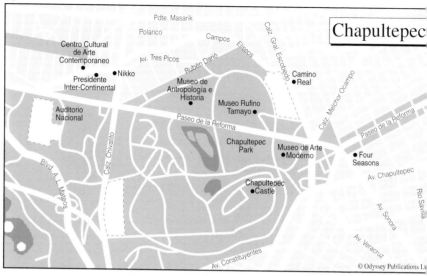

Pdte. Masarik

Polanco

Campos

Calz. Gral. Escobedo

Elíseos

Centro Cultural
de Arte
Contemporaneo

Av. Tres Picos

Rubén Darío

Camino
● Real

Calz. Melchor Ocampo

● Nikko

Presidente
Inter-Continental

Museo de
Antropología e
Historia

Museo Rufino
Tamayo ●

Paseo de la Reforma

Auditorio
Nacional

Calz. Chivatito

Paseo de la Reforma

Four
Seasons

Chapultepec
Park

Museo de Arte
● Moderno

Av. Chapultepec

Blvd. A. L. Mateos

Rio Savilla

Chapultepec
● Castle

Av. Sonora

Av. Veracruz

Av. Constituyentes

Chapultepec

© Odyssey Publications Lt

and frequently march to protest at the feet of Columbus. A half block north of Reforma on **Avenida Insurgentes**, the major north–south artery and the city's longest avenue, lies the **Parque Sullivan**. This small park, just west of the massive **Monument to the Mother**, is the site of a popular open-air art show and sale on Sunday mornings. Two blocks south of the Cuauhtémoc statue on Calle Dinamarca is the **Wax Museum**, 6 Calle Londres. Among the highlights are the Mexican and international historical figures, the Mexican movie stars and, in the basement, the delightfully tacky Chamber of Horrors. Next door is the **Museo Ripley**, associated with the Ripley's Believe It or Not Organization. Admission is N$30 for adults and N$20 for children, students and certified teachers.

Just to the west, the neighborhood bounded by Reforma, Insurgentes, Av Chapultepec and Calle Sevilla is the famous **Zona Rosa** ('Pink Zone'). This district has pretensions of being Mexico City's equivalent of Montparnasse in Paris or New York's Greenwich Village. Unfortunately, the cultural and bohemian aspects of those neighborhoods are nowhere to be found, since all that abounds are glitzy shops and nightlife. Expensive hotels and excellent restaurants, many open air, are also found here. Calles Hamburgo and Londres are the Zona Rosa's main streets; Calle Amberes contains many upscale crafts and jewelry stores and art galleries, while Calle Génova is lined with boutiques aimed at the teenage market. Across Reforma, the massive **United States Embassy** occupies the block between Calles Rio Sena and Rio Danubio; the line of people seeking visas is frequently blocks long. A block west stands the **Monument to Independence** (1909), 40 meters (130 feet) tall from street level to the golden *Angel of Independence*, one of Mexico City's most beloved sculptures. The base of the column contains the severed head of Miguel Hidalgo, the priest who initiated Mexico's fight for independence, as well as the remains of Morelos, Allende and other heroes of the Insurgency. In 1957, a severe earthquake toppled the angel, but it was restored and the monument reinforced. Reforma's next and last traffic circle holds the **Fountain of Diana the Huntress**, recently moved from near Chapultepec Park. The statue represents a goddess who is not a robed, sylph-like huntress but a naked voluptuous damsel who more closely conforms to the Latin American ideal of womanhood. Six blocks further on, Reforma arrives at Chapultepec Park.

Grasshopper Hill

Originally situated on the western shore of the valley's great lake system, Chapultepec, which means 'Hill of the Grasshopper' in Nahuatl, has long been revered by inhabitants. This hill was the Aztec's first home in the valley when they arrived from the north around AD 1300. After they founded Tenochtitlán and conquered the valley, the hill's springs fed water to the city via long aqueducts, and its rocks were carved into great monuments of Aztec leaders. The Aztec kings built palaces on Chapultepec and the surrounding lands became their gardens. The Spanish razed the palaces and turned the hill into a park in which nobles hunted for wild game. In 1841, Chapultepec Castle was built on the top of the hill and became the home of the Military College. When the American army invaded Mexico City in 1847, the castle was the last bastion of opposition; six military cadets, now enshrined as the *Niños Héroes* ('Heroic Boys'), flung themselves from the ramparts rather than surrender. The Emperor Maximilian converted the castle into a palatial residence, and after his short, unhappy reign it became the Military College again. In this century, it housed Mexico's presidents until 1940, when it was given to the Mexican people as a museum. Today **Chapultepec Park** is one of the most charming spots in the city and fills every weekend with picnicking families. It is also the best place to get respite from the relentless traffic and pollution—if only Mexico City had more green lungs like this!

The main park gates are just after Reforma bends to the right on its way up to the Lomas de Chapultepec neighborhood and the Toluca highway beyond. The first sight is the **Monument to the Niños Héroes**; each of the six massive columns contains the remains of one of the cadets who committed suicide on 13 September 1847 rather than surrender to the Americans. Just to the right stands the **Museo de Arte Moderno** (entrance on the north side; Tues–Sun, 11 am–6 pm). The kidney-shaped, modernist main building (1964) contains an interior dome with remarkable sound-magnifying properties. The permanent collection includes paintings by well-known 20th-century masters like Frida Kahlo, José Clemente Orozco, David Alfaro Siquieros and

Dr Atl, as well as less famous and more recent abstracts. Good temporary exhibitions are often housed here and in the smaller, circular Galería Fernando Gamboa, which may be reached through the sculpture garden.

Behind the *Niños Héroes* monument, a road winds up Chapultepec Hill to **Chapultepec Castle**. A small building just to the north of this ramp is filled with **funhouse mirrors** (nominal fee), which incite screams of fright and recognition from young and old. There is no bus or cable car service up to the castle; you have to walk, so take it slow. Near the top you come to the **Galería del Museo Nacional de Historia** (Tues–Sun, 9 am–5 pm), also known as the Caracol or 'snail' from its shape. The spiral-shaped exhibition gallery inside tells the story of Mexico's fight for independence from the late colonial era through the Revolution, with maps, dioramas and reproductions. It actually resembles an extended, occasionally three-dimensional cartoon. A silver case at the foot of the exhibition contains a copy of the 1917 Constitution.

A few steps further on stands Chapultepec Castle, now the **Museo Nacional de Historia** (Tues–Sun, 9 am–5 pm), which contains many unique artefacts from Mexican history and patriotic murals by famous artists like Orozco and Siquieros. The building itself is mostly the product of Emperor Maximilian's renovations and expansions, although Díaz and subsequent presidents also initiated renovations. Among the highlights of the museum are Siquieros's mural of the Revolution, which fills a room just to the left of the entrance. Jorge Camareno's mural, *The Fusion of Two Cultures*, shows an Aztec eagle warrior and a Spanish knight locked in battle while the new nation, in the form of an eagle, is born in flames. *Reform and the Fall of the Empire* by José Clemente Orozco depicts the evil forces of mid-19th-century conservatism and foreign intervention—priests, generals and Maximilian—being menaced by a huge, floating colossal head of President Juárez. Here also is Miguel Cabrera's celebrated portrait of the baroque poetess, Sor Juana Inés de la Cruz, surrounded by volumes representing her prodigious learning. The museum's well-organized galleries tell the story of colonial Mexico through exhibitions on evangelization, the economy, food and art. You may see Maximilian and Carlota's private apartments on the second floor of the north wing. There is also a good bookstore here. If the pollution is not too dense, there is a view of the city from the gardens surrounding the castle.

Returning to the foot of the hill, a short walk north of the Museo de Arte Moderno and across Reforma brings you to the **Museo Rufino Tamayo** (Tues–Sun, 10 am–6 pm). This bunker-like 1981 museum contains the modern art collection (Max Ernst, Andy Warhol, Willem de Kooning, et al) of this Oaxacan-born painter (1899–1991), as well as a permanent collection of his own work. One of these is his amusing portrait of *El Rockanrolero*. Looming just to the west is Mexico's largest and most

Aztec Sacrifice

All Mesoamerican cultures practiced human sacrifice. Archeologists have found evidence of sacrificial victims in settlements of Puebla's Tehuacan Valley dated 9000–7000 BC. In Veracruz, the Indians of the Huastec Culture and those of El Tajín ritually decapitated the losers in their sacred ball games. The Classic Maya aristocracy tortured and killed captives to legitimate and make sacred their claims to power. However, it was the Aztecs who made human sacrifice the central ritual of their culture—it literally made the world go round—and killed far more people than perhaps all earlier cultures combined. The Spanish were horrified by these 'barbaric' practices and stamping them out became a justification of the Conquest. Until this century, however, nobody ever looked beyond the horror and investigated what place the ritual actually had in religious and political belief.

Human sacrifice was a common ritual among the Aztecs. Every major god had regular sacrificial rites in his or her honor, and the priests devised different ways of killing people for each rite, including shooting with arrows, decapitation, pushing them off a wooden tower and flaying them alive. The victims were usually the least powerful in the culture—prisoners of war, women and children, although sometimes the women and children were taken from the noble class. The most frequent sacrificial rites were those in honor of the rain god Tláloc, whose goodwill was crucial for the success of the crops. By far the most notorious were those performed in honor of the main Aztec deity, Huitzilopochtli, the god of the sun and of war. These were the sacrifices the Conquistadors witnessed—and sometimes were victims of—while attempting to capture Tenochtitlán. The Spanish also heard rumors of a great rite in the not-too-distant past in which more than 80,000 prisoners had been killed in a ceremony in honor of the reconstruction of the Templo Mayor.

The sacrifices to Huitzilopochtli began with a number of ceremonies as the prisoners-of-war, the preferred victims, were led to the temple-pyramid. At the rite's climax, the parade of prisoners was led up the steps to the shrine of Huitzilopochtli, where a waist-high stone stood in front of the temple holding the great stone image of the god. Each was met by a team of six blood-stained priests. Five, dressed in white and black, grabbed him by his limbs and neck and splayed him belly-up on a pointed waist-high stone. A stone yoke was placed on his neck, bending him back, while the sixth priest approached with a razor-sharp obsidian knife. He plunged the knife into the prisoner's abdomen, reached in and pulled out his heart, which he displayed to the sun, and then placed in the stone Huitzilopochtli's hollowed-out mouth. The five priests threw the lifeless body down the stairs, drenching them with blood. The sacrifice was probably over in less than a minute. Down below, the warrior who had captured the prisoner carried off the body to be butchered and ritually eaten.

It is a subject of debate of how many people were actually killed in these ceremonies. The 80,000 death toll mentioned above comes from Aztec accounts of the five-day ceremony celebrating the expansion of the Great Temple in 1487 (every 52 years it had to be rebuilt, and masses of prisoners were killed in its honor). Anthropologists believe that this number is almost certainly an exaggeration meant to impress the gods and strike fear in the hearts of their enemies. Not only is it logistically nearly impossible (they would have had to kill one prisoner every five seconds to finish them all in five days), but it would have decimated the surrounding armies for decades afterward—not a good idea if you need a constant flow of prisoners. Researchers believe that a figure of 20,000—still shocking to our sensibilities—is nearer to the truth.

While their other gods were also found throughout Mesoamerica, Huitzilopochtli, their guardian deity, was unique to the Aztecs. Why did they find it necessary to sacrifice so copiously in his honor? The symbolism of these ceremonies is readily apparent. They were re-enactments of Huitzilopochtli's mythic battle with his 400 brothers, in which he slew his sister, Coyolxauhqui, and threw her dismembered body down the hillside. The Aztecs believed that this battle was replayed every night, as the sun god fought the gods of the night, his brothers, so that day might come. The hearts and blood of prisoners-of-war were the food and drink that fueled his strength. Casting the bodies down the steps re-enacted his sister's fall; the Coyolxauhqui stone depicting her broken body was buried in front of the Great Temple's steps. Thus, if the Aztecs did not sacrifice, eternal night would fall and their world would come to an end.

Beyond the symbolic level, why was it necessary for the Aztecs to kill such a large number of people, particularly prisoners-of-war, on a regular basis? The Aztec state was not monolithic; anthropologists believe that there were profound tensions between the warrior-rulers associated with Huitzilopochtli and the more peaceful priestly castes devoted to Tláloc, the

continues

rain god. Hence the duality of the Great Temple, where the two gods shared their position at the center of the Aztec universe. In order to justify their control, the warrior-rulers instituted a policy of continuous expansion of the Aztec state coupled with fervent worship of Huitzilopochtli. The warriors told their people that they needed to wage constant war, not because they were threatened from without, but because they needed an unending stream of prisoners-of-war in order that their principal deity might win his battle with the gods of the night. The universe would collapse without it. What better reason for bloodshed?

Recently, some anthropologists have speculated that there were hidden sub-texts to Aztec human sacrifices beneath the politico-religious explanation. The two most prominent theories are that the Aztecs killed and ate humans to make up for a protein deficiency and that mass sacrifice was a means of population control. However, there is no evidence of a protein deficiency in Aztec remains, and they had numerous other protein sources, including specially bred dogs. The Aztecs did eat their victims but only in small amounts and ritualistically. They would have had to butcher many more for the populace to receive significant nutritional gains. As for population control, killing crowds of males, particularly foreign males, was tremendously inefficient, because women's child-bearing capabilities remained as strong as ever.

Another subject of (macabre) speculation is how they actually performed the sacrifices. The Spanish eyewitness accounts tell of the priest simply plunging the knife into the victim's breast and pulling the heart out with his hand. A heart surgeon, Dr Francis Robicsek, has pointed out that this is easier said than done. The heart is the best-protected organ after the brain, and the victim probably did not make the rite any easier by struggling. There are many ways to reach the heart—splitting the breast bone, breaking through the ribs, penetrating diagonally up from the abdomen—but most are time-consuming, sloppy and increase the chances of damaging the organ. A sacrifice is, after all, a religious ceremony and should be conducted with the proper decorum and grace. Based on his surgical experience, Dr Robicsek decided that the most likely method is a 'transverse bilateral thoracotomy'. Using a wide and serrated obsidian blade that was probably sharper than a surgeon's scalpel, the priest cut horizontally across the victim's rib cage, causing a large wound that gaped open due to the body's bent-backward position. The victim's lungs collapsed, stopping his struggles, and the heart was easily exposed and extracted by cutting the major veins and arteries with a knife-like obsidian blade.

The last question is why the Aztec people tolerated mass human sacrifice. Why did they not rise up and overthrow their priests and rulers? Aztec culture was very different from our own. First, sacrifice was traditional; it was practiced by every earlier culture they took inspiration from, including the Teotihuacanos, Toltecs, Huastecs and Mayas. Western beliefs about the sanctity of the individual were non-existent— one Spanish writer compared Tenochtitlán to an ant colony— and death was viewed not as the end of life but its continuation. The Aztecs almost certainly felt some measure of horror at the sacrifices, but it was tempered by religious joy. They saw life on Earth as at best a transitory state and at worst as a

Pyramid at Tenayuca

kind of living hell of constant upheaval and turmoil. The sacrificial victims were blessed, because they became the gods in whose honor they died, and their souls traveled to an Aztec paradise. And, most importantly, the deaths were in the name of a greater good: to keep the Sun on its course and the rain falling on the crops. It also should be noted that certain Spanish customs, like burning heretics and branding slaves on the cheek, were just as horrific to the Aztecs as human sacrifice is to us.

celebrated museum, the **Museo Nacional de Antropología** (Tues–Sat, 9 am–7 pm; Sun, 10 am–6 pm). Here, one of the world's greatest archeological collections is housed in a stunning 1964 building designed by Pedro Ramírez Vázquez. At the entrance stands a 7-meter (23-foot) tall statue supposedly representing Tláloc, the pre-Columbian rain god, which was found in a hillside northeast of the city. The museum's interior patio is shaded by an enormous rectangular roof held up by one massive carved column that also spouts water from the top. A day or even two should be set aside to see the museum properly. At the entrance there is a good bookstore, a theater and a hall for temporary exhibitions; a cafeteria occupies the basement.

The first floor is devoted to the archeology of pre-Hispanic cultures, while the second contains ethnographic exhibitions on nearly all of Mexico's present-day Indian tribes, including the Purepechans, Otomis, Totonacs, Nahuas, Mixtecs, Huastecs and Mayas. Unfortunately all the labels are in Spanish (good English guidebooks are available in the bookstore) and many, especially in the Maya room, are woefully out of date. The Aztecs occupy the largest and most central room, even though other cultures, like the Maya, had greater achievements; the Nobel prize-winning poet, Octavio Paz, believes that this is intended as a subtle justification of Mexico City's hegemony over the rest of the country. Here is a hall-by-hall tour of the first floor exhibitions:

Sala I: Introduction to anthropology, evolution, language and world cultures

Sala II: Introduction to Mesoamerica

Sala III: Origins of Man in Mesoamerica, early agriculture, the Santa Isabel Iztapán mammoth bones

Sala IV: Pre-Classical cultures around the Valley of Mexico, including a Tlatilco burial excavation and a reproduction of an Olmec relief from Chalcatzingo

Sala V: Teotihuacán, with a diorama of the city, a reproduction of the Temple of Queztlacoatl, a sculpture of Xipe Totec ('The Flayed God') and a case of jade- and turquoise-encrusted stone masks

Sala VI: The Toltecs in Xochicalco, with a relief from the Temple of the Feathered Serpent, and Tula, represented by the giant warrior columns

Sala VII: The Mexica, better known as the Aztecs, occupy the museum's focal point; here are a diorama of Tenochtitlán, incredible sculptures of Coatlicue and Xiuhcoatl and, of course, the famous Calendar Stone, also known as the Sun Stone

Sala VIII: Oaxaca, including the *Danzantes* ('Dancers'—probably dead captive chieftains) and a mock-up of the treasure-laden Tomb 104, both from Monte Albán

Sala IX: The Gulf of Mexico, with an Olmec colossal head from San Lorenzo, jade burial offerings from La Venta, the famous stone wrestler' and Totonac artefacts from El Tajín

Sala X: The Maya, starting with an introduction to their culture; artefacts include portrait funeral ceramics from Jaina Island, Palenque's Temple of the Cross relief and Temple of the Inscription crypt holding the bones of Lord Pacal; outside are reproductions of the Edificio of Ho chob from Campeche and the Bonampak murals

Sala XI: Northern Mexico desert and Chichimec cultures, including sites in the Bajo and Casas Grandes in Chihuahua

Sala XII: West Mexico, with many astonishing figurines from Tomb Culture burials, together with Tarascan artefacts from Michoacán

Two blocks north of the museum stands the **Sala de Arte Público Siquieros** (Mon–Fri, 10 am–5 pm; Sat, 10 am–1 pm), 29 Av Tres Picos, which was the muralist and revolutionary's home. It has been converted into a museum of his art, with photos of many of his murals and a number of smaller oil paintings.

Nearby stands the **Centro Cultural de Arte Contemporáneo** (admission: N$5 for adults; N$2.50 for students and certified teachers; on Tuesdays children under 12 and students free; on weekends, general public free), at the corner of Campos Eliseos and Jorge Eliot next to the Hotel Presidente. This is the museum of the television giant Televisa's cultural foundations. Three floors of exhibitions include their permanent collections of pre-Columbian and modern art as well as many high-quality traveling exhibits.

South of the Anthropology Museum across Reforma you find the **Zoological Garden**, the **Botanical Garden**, a **children's amusement park** and a lake with rowboats for rent. On weekends the paths are lined with vendors selling an incredible variety of balloons, toys and snack foods. The enormous **Auditorio Nacional**, west of the zoo and across Reforma from the Hotel Presidente Chapultepec skyscraper, is the site of performances by top Mexican and international musical artists. Hidden behind the trees at the south side of the park is **Los Pinos**, the official residence of the president of Mexico. Chapultepec Park continues west of Blvd Manuel Avila Camacho with the **adult amusement park**, a modern **Technology Museum** filled with interactive exhibits, and a rather run-down **Natural History Museum** housed in four tent-like structures. West of the amusement park is a major pumping station for the city's water supply, which has been turned into a series of attractive fountains with mosaics and murals by Diego Rivera.

Anthropology Museum roof

Just beyond the Periferico highway, the westernmost portion of Chapultepec is home to the new Papalote **Children's Museum**. A short walk from the Constituyentes metro station, this remarkable museum contains 250 interactive exhibits, an IMAX theater and excellent temporary exhibitions. All of this is housed in a striking, light-flooded building meant to evoke a *papalote*, or 'kite'. Be warned that the museum is closed for lunch from 1–2 pm on weekdays and 2–3 pm at weekends. Further west, this part of Chapultepec is home to a huge cemetery, a riding academy, public swimming pools and the city's largest *charro* (Mexican rodeo) arena. The neighborhoods north of the park, particularly Lomas de Chapultepec, are the city's ritziest. Forbidding walls hide huge mansions with armed guards at many entrances.

The North

Reforma heads north from the Alameda to **Ciudad Tlatelolco**, an enormous housing project that begins just northwest of the **Monument to Cuitláhuac**, the penultimate Aztec king. Many of Tlatelolco's apartment buildings were severely damaged or destroyed by the 1985 earthquake and remain empty. Shortly after the founding of Tenochtitlán, conditions on the island community became so crowded that a group set off to build a town on another island a few kilometers to the northwest. This was named Tlatelolco, which means something like 'built-up mound of earth'. Its residents founded another dynasty here and became known as the consummate traders of Mesoamerica, exchanging luxury goods as far away as Guatemala. As the Aztec

The Adolescent, *Huaxtec region sculpture, Anthropology Museum*

empire spread, its vanguard was Tlatelolco merchants who combined trading with spying for the Aztec armies. Tlatelolco was home to the empire's largest market, filled with domesticated and wild animals, fruits, vegetables, medicinal herbs, slaves and luxury goods. When the conquistadors visited it, they were awed by its richness and diversity. Tlatelolco was also the final Aztec stronghold against the Spanish. On 13 August 1521, Cuauhtémoc, the last Aztec king and son of Cuitláhuac, was captured near here, signalling that the conquistadors had defeated the great warrior empire and begun a new era for Mesoamerica.

The remains of the market, a ball court and a pyramid, now called the **Plaza de las Tres Culturas**, lie one block northwest of the Cuitláhuac traffic circle. The Spanish razed the Aztec buildings, so all that is visible are some walls and foundations. Archeologists believe that the twin-staircased pyramid, which was rebuilt 11 times, greatly resembled the one at Tenayuca in the north of the city. A plaque commemorates Cuauhtémoc's capture and avers: 'It was not a triumph nor a defeat, it was the painful birth of the mixed race that is Mexico today'. The **Iglesia de Santiago** was erected overlooking the ruins in 1524 (rebuilt 1609); its austere, single-vaulted interior is notable for a huge fresco of St Christopher over the side door. The **Colegio de San Buenaventura** (1779) next door was built as a Franciscan school for the sons of Aztec nobles. The third culture, modern Mexico, is represented by the headquarters of the Secretariat of Foreign Relations along the south side of the plaza.

Just north of Ciudad Tlatelolco, Reforma divides in two and becomes Calz de Guadalupe (northbound) and Calz de los Misterios (southbound), both of which terminate about three kilometers further on at the **Villa de Guadalupe**, Mexico's holiest shrine. A walkway up the center of Calz de Guadalupe is the pilgrimage path of the faithful, some shuffling forward on their knees, on their way to the shrine. In 1531, a Christianized Indian named Juan Diego had a vision of the Virgin Mary dressed in the clothes of an Indian on the hill of Tepeyac. Not coincidentally, the Aztecs worshipped at a shrine to Tonantzin, the mother god, on the same hill. The Virgin Mary told Juan Diego to go to Bishop Zumárraga and tell him to build a shrine in her honor. Juan Diego was too scared to obey until she gave him a bouquet of roses, which were out of season, and told him to take them to the bishop as proof. When Juan Diego opened his cloak to show the bishop the roses, the bishop saw that a beautiful dark-skinned image of the Virgin had appeared on the cloak's lining. The shrine to the Virgin of Guadalupe was quickly built and her image became central to the Spanish campaign to convert the Indians. Juan Diego was recently canonized by Pope John Paul II.

The current **basilica** (1976) is a huge and ugly concrete building (designed by Pedro Ramírez Vázquez, who was also the architect for the Anthropology Museum), which holds over 20,000 people. The original cloak hangs behind bulletproof glass above the altar and may be seen by stepping on a conveyor belt behind the altar and passing under it. Enthusiastic researchers have discovered that the image becomes younger and purer-looking with the passing years and that her eyes actually contain the tiny silhouettes of the Apostles, as if they were caught by a camera. Some of the pilgrims are poor peasants who have walked from towns hundreds of miles away. On major religious holidays, particularly the Virgin's holy days of December 11th and 12th, the shrine is jammed with tens of thousands. The original basilica, the baroque **Iglesia de Guadalupe** (1704–25), stands just northeast of the new building and is now a religious museum with many votive offerings and a collection of church treasures that includes a stupendous solid-silver altarpiece. A path winds up the hill to the **Iglesia del Cerrito** and then to the **Capilla del Pocito**, a circular chapel that encloses a well. There is also a look-out with a fine view over the polluted city. Photographers with painted backdrops let you have your picture taken with the Virgin as a souvenir of your visit. A covered **market** just to the east is filled with hundreds of vendors selling all manner of religious artefacts, from jewelry to life-size sculptures of saints.

Lovers of archeology will want to continue north just across the border of the State

A painful pilgrimage to the shrine of Guadalupe, Enrique Díaz

of Mexico, where Tenayuca and Santa Cecilia Acatitlán lie, two small but well-preserved sites. To reach them, head north on Eje Central Lázaro Cárdenas to where it turns into Av Acueducto-Tenayuca. Turn right at Av Pirámide, where Calz Vallejo enters from the left, and **Tenayuca** is half a block on the right. You may also take *peseros* here from the Basilica and La Raza metro

Votive offerings to the Virgin of Guadalupe

stations. Before the arrival of the Aztecs, Tenayuca, which means 'the place where walls are made', was an important Chichimec settlement. Archeologists believe that some Tenayucans may have helped found Tlatelolco, because the pyramids at both sites are so similar. Tenayuca's rectangular pyramid, one of the best preserved in the area, is surrounded on three sides by hundreds of stone serpent heads, some with red pigment still visible in their mouths. Four earlier pyramids were found inside this structure. To the north lie two small platforms with a round serpent sculpture between them. The small museum on the grounds was closed indefinitely at the time of writing. Tenayuca's little parish church stands just south of the ruins and contains a *mudéjar* wooden ceiling and a crude baroque altar. Early graffiti may be seen carved into some of the stones around the entrance.

The ruins of **Santa Cecilia Acatitlán** lie about half a kilometer (third of a mile) north of Tenayuca on Av Piramide (follow the signs). Another Chichimec construction, Santa Cecilia's pyramid, has been reconstructed with a temple on top. The neighboring church was built with stones from pre-Hispanic temples. The hills beyond these two sites are covered with shanties clinging to the steep slopes—home for the thousands of recent immigrants from Mexico's poverty-stricken rural areas to the capital.

The South

Avenida Insurgentes is the city's longest street, running 25 kilometers (15.5miles) from the Pachuca highway in the north all the way to the Cuernavaca highway in the south. After crossing Reforma and Av Chapultepec, Insurgentes is lined with modern office buildings and upscale restaurants and nightclubs as it heads downtown. At the corner of Calle Filadelfia stands the skeleton of the 50-story **Hotel Mexico**, recently renamed the 'World Trade Center', which is one of the country's tallest buildings. It has remained unfinished since the owner ran out of money, but a popular revolving restaurant and nightclub is open on the top floor. In front of this edifice is the eccentric 12-sided **Siquieros Polyforum**, designed by the artist David Alfaro Siquieros and covered with wild murals. The octagonal interior contains exhibition spaces, theaters, a craft store and a huge three-dimensional mural by Siquieros that mixes sculpture and painting; it is called *The March of Humanity on Earth and Toward the Cosmos*. About seven blocks south, Eje 6 Sur (Calle Holbein) turns west to the 100,000-seat **Olympic Soccer Stadium** and the **Plaza México** bullfighting arena, supposedly the world's largest with seating for 64,000. During the winter season bullfights are staged at 4 pm on Sundays. The **Parque Hundido**, three blocks south, contains a clock decorated with flowers and a garden displaying reproductions of famous pre-Columbian monuments from Mexico's museums. The façade of the **Teatro Insurgentes** at the corner of Calle Mercaderes, about a kilometer (0.6 miles) south, is decorated with a huge mosaic (1951–53) by Diego Rivera entitled *The History of Theater in Mexico*. It depicts the Mexican comic, Cantinflas, taking from the rich and giving to the poor, Juárez and Zapata in the left- and right-hand corners, and a large figure in the foreground holding its forehead as if in pain. It is not considered Rivera's best or most coherent work.

SAN ANGEL

The charming neighborhood of San Angel occupies an area that was originally Chimalistac, an Aztec town, and a smaller settlement called Tenanitla. After the Conquest, it bordered the property of a prominent Indian convert named Juan de Guzmán, who deeded his lands to various religious orders on his death. With the founding of two wealthy convents, San Angel became a center of religious learning and Mexico City's élite began to flock here on weekends. The friars planted huge gardens of agricultural and decorative plants from Spain; from here the plants spread throughout Mexico, permanently transforming life with the kind of efficacy of which governments can only dream. San Angel was a village until the early 20th century, when new roads and trolley lines extended the reach of the city. When the old élite either were destroyed by the Revolution or moved to enclaves like Lomas de Chapultepec, artists and intellectuals occupied their mansions. This 'intellectual tendency' was reinforced by the construction of UNAM's University City just to the south in the 1950s. San Angel is one of the last places in the city where you can walk on quiet, tree-lined cobblestone streets and get a sense of what life was like before the industrial era.

After crossing Av Miguel Angel de Quevedo, Insurgentes enters the **San Angel** neighborhood. About two blocks east on Quevedo stands the **Librería Gandhi**, one of Mexico City's largest bookstores. Its second floor café is a popular gathering spot for local academics and writers. The **Jardín de Bonilla** just after Av Quevedo contains the **Álvaro Obregón Monument**, which was built on the site of the restaurant where this Mexican president was assassinated by a fanatic Cristero caricaturist in 1928. The arm that Obregón lost in a 1915 battle used to float in a glass jar of formaldehyde on a shelf inside the monument. The arm was recently returned to his family and cremated, but the jar, filled with murky fluid, is still visible! The **Capilla de San Sebastián Mártir** in a small park just to the east is a small, but charming, baroque chapel with a churrigueresque altar and frescoes depicting the life of the saint. The surrounding park was the site of the colonial gardens mentioned above. Av La Paz climbs the hill on the other side of Insurgentes to the heart of San Angel. The **Convento del Carmen** to the left on Av Revolución was founded in 1613 by the Carmelite order and was one of the most luxurious in the Mexico City area. Its library contained 12,000 volumes, and in the 17th century it may have been the largest in the New World. Many of these riches are preserved in the **Museo del Carmen** (Tues–Sun, 10 am–5 pm) housed in the old convent. Inside are frescoed walls, 17th-century religious paintings, fine furniture and *mudéjar*-style wooden ceilings on the second floor. For Mexican tourists, the most popular attraction is the 12 mummified monks in glass-topped cases housed in the basement crypt. The **convent church** next door has a tiled dome and a churrigueresque altar inside. The largest of the interior chapels contains three interesting tile altars under scalloped half-domes. A smaller chapel on the left houses a retable filled with reliquaries. The **Centro Cultural San Angel** across Av Revolución houses temporary art exhibitions and a café.

A block up the hill on Calle Madero takes you to the gracious **Plaza San Jacinto**

Matador and bull, Mexico City

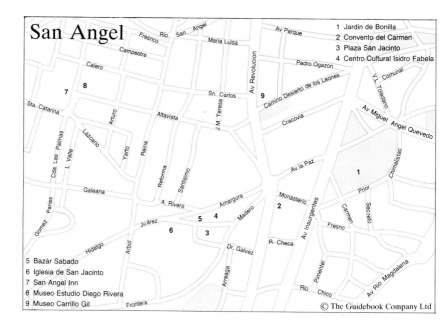

San Angel

1 Jardín de Bonilla
2 Convento del Carmen
3 Plaza San Jacinto
4 Centro Cultural Isidro Fabela
5 Bazár Sabado
6 Iglesia de San Jacinto
7 San Angel Inn
8 Museo Estudio Diego Rivera
9 Museo Carrillo Gil

© The Guidebook Company Ltd

lined with low-key restaurants and gift shops. A 1681 mansion on the north side of the plaza is now the **Centro Cultural Isidro Fabela** (free), which contains an impressive collection of European and Mexican painting and sculpture from the 15th to the 19th centuries. This collection, donated by Fabela, a famous writer, lawyer and diplomat, seems to be rarely visited, but it as good as better-known museums in the city center. On Saturdays, another old mansion a few doors to the west hosts the **Bazar Sábado**, a famous crafts market that attracts busloads of tourists.

Continuing west a half block, you come to the Dominican **Iglesia de San Jacinto** (late 16th century), whose beautiful courtyard always seems to be filled with art students. Inside the simple renaissance façade is a single-vaulted nave and a gilt altarpiece. The chapel on the left is decorated with paintings of the saint's martyrdom. San Angel's cobblestone side streets are lined with beautiful colonial mansions behind huge stone walls.

A short downhill walk to the north will bring you to Av Altavista, which is lined with fancy clothing, chocolate and interior decorating stores discretely set in small shopping centers. The **Antigua Hacienda de Goycoechea** at Altavista's west end was once a favorite resting spot for General Santa Ana. Now it is the **San Angel Inn**, one of the finest and most expensive traditional restaurants in the city. Even if you do not eat there, it is worth a visit just to see the grounds. Just across the street stands the

Museo Estudio Diego Rivera, a modernist 1933 house designed by Juan O'Gorman that was the muralist's studio for many years. From the practical point of view, the house is distinctly uncomfortable; it is hard to see how the portly Rivera could have tolerated the tiny bedroom or navigated up the narrow spiral staircase. The most interesting room is the large studio, still cluttered with his collections of folk and pre-Hispanic art and his painting equipment. Some of his portraits, including one of Dolores del Río with large, Walter Keane-ish eyes, are displayed on the easels. Returning down Altavista to Av Revolución, diagonally across the intersection stands the **Museo Carrillo Gil**, another modernist building housing the modern art collection—the best in Mexico City—of Carrillo Gil, a Mexican artist. The first floor is devoted to temporary exhibitions; on the second is the largest collection of paintings of José Clemente Orozco, and the third contains paintings from Rivera's early cubist period, as well as work by Siquieros, Picasso, Roualt and Carrillo Gil himself. There is also a good art bookstore on the first floor.

Av Altavista heading west becomes Calz Desierto de los Leones and ends at the **Parque Nacional Desierto de los Leones** ('Desert of the Lions'), which is not a desert at all but a pine-forested hill 22 kilometers (14 miles) west of the city. A Carmelite convent, built here in the early 17th century, became a Zapatista stronghold during the Revolution. City residents come for the fresh air; visit the convent and picnic or eat in one of the popular restaurants.

COYOACÁN

Three kilometers (two miles) to the east of San Angel on Av Miguel Angel de Quevedo lies the heart of Coyoacán, another suburb filled with attractive colonial buildings. Coyoacán, with an important freshwater spring, was one of the earliest pre-Hispanic settlements on the shores of the Valley of Mexico's network of lakes. By the 13th century, it was populated by the Tepanecs, who had arrived in the valley shortly before the Aztecs. The settlement remained independent of the Aztecs until the early 15th century, when King Itzcóatl claimed that the Tepanecs had raped and robbed Aztec women and ordered an attack on Coyoacán. From this lakeside town, a great causeway was built that linked Tenochtitlán with its empire to the south. After the Conquest, Cortés made the attractive town his capital while the devastated Tenochtitlán was being rebuilt and many of his captains built houses here. During the colonial era the town became a weekend retreat for the Spanish élite, and Coyoacán's chief, who hated the Aztecs, converted to Christianity, taking the name of Juan de Guzmán. Most of his town belonged to Cortés' estate, of which Guzmán was overseer, and he also became an important property owner in his own right. Guzmán assiduously courted the favor, and the business, of the colonial government; by 1550 he may have been one of the richest men in Mexico. He was so confident of his stature that he

Colonial style house

actually sued the Cortés family for payment of services rendered. The suit was not settled in his lifetime, but he and his heirs left a lasting mark by donating land to religious orders to build convents in nearby San Angel. Like that suburb, Coyoacán was a village until the 20th century, when new transit lines brought the city to its door. The 'death' of the old Coyoacán had been heralded since the 1930s, but today it is famous as the home of many prominent artists, politicians and intellectuals.

Coyoacán's main square is the attractive **Plaza Hidalgo**, five blocks north of Miguel Angel de Quevedo on Calle Felipe Carrillo Puerto. The north side of the square is occupied by the one-story **Casa de Cortés** (16th century), which now contains offices of the municipal government. This house is said to be the spot where Cortés tortured Cuauhtémoc to force him to reveal the location of the Aztec treasure, and also where Cortés murdered his Spanish wife with his bare hands. Anti-Spanish murals by Diego Rivera decorate the interior. The **Iglesia de San Juan Bautista** across the plaza was begun in 1552, and heavily reconstructed in 1804 and 1929. The glory of the original décor can be seen to the left of the altar in the **Capilla del Sagrario**, with a very impressive baroque retable and elaborate solomonic columns. The chapel also houses a much-adored gold reliquary. A half block to the east on Av Hidalgo stands the **Museo Nacional de Culturas Populares**, which has exhibitions on such amusing subjects as old radio shows, circuses and professional wrestling. The **Capilla de la Concepción** (18th century) on the pretty little **Plaza de la Conchita**, two blocks southeast of Plaza Hidalgo, contains ornate gilt retables. A short walk five blocks north of the plaza takes you to the fascinating **Frida Kahlo Museum** (Tues–Sun, 10 am–2 pm, 3 pm–6 pm). This was the house and studio of Kahlo, the artist who is now a cult figure, and her lover Diego Rivera; it is preserved as they left it. The rooms are filled with their art collection, folk and archeological artefacts, as well as interesting personal possessions like the bed Kahlo spent years in as an invalid and the painting she was working on when she died—a portrait of Stalin. A few blocks away at 45 Calle Viena stands the fortified home-in-exile of the Russian communist **Leon Trotsky**, who was murdered here by a Stalinist agent in 1940. The building is now a **museum** (Tues–Fri, 10.30 am–2 pm, 3 pm–5 pm; Sat–Sun, 1 pm–4 pm) manned by Trotskyite volunteers from around the world, and you can see Trotsky's grave, the bullet holes in the walls from an earlier unsuccessful assassination attempt (led by the muralist Siquieros) and Trotsky's desk as he left it on the day of his death.

Calle Xicoténcatl four blocks south of the museum will take you east across Av Div del Norte to the **Convento de Churubusco**, now the **Museum of the Interventions**. In pre-Hispanic times, a temple to Huitzilopochtli, the main Aztec deity, stood here. The convent was completed in 1590. In 1849, the thick-walled structure was occupied by the Mexican army, who fought a bloody battle here against the advancing Americans. They were helped by Irish deserters from the US army who were captured during the battle and condemned to death; they are now lionized as Mexican heroes. The ornate, frescoed interior now houses the Museum of the Interventions, a history of the many, many times that foreign forces, including French, Texans, mercenaries, Native Americans from north of the border and, of course, the United States Government, invaded Mexico. Among the many interesting historical artefacts on display is the throne used by the Emperor Iturbide. The convent is also home to the Centro de Restauración, a government workshop where antiquities, both pre-Hispanic and colonial, are restored. Just to the east are the huge

Intricately carved door-knocker

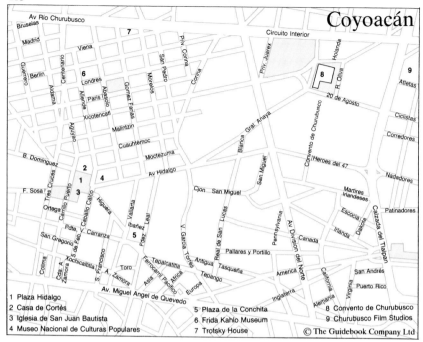

Coyoacán

1 Plaza Hidalgo
2 Casa de Cortés
3 Iglesia de San Juan Bautista
4 Museo Nacional de Culturas Populares
5 Plaza de la Conchita
6 Frida Kahlo Museum
7 Trotsky House
8 Convento de Churubusco
9 Churubusco Film Studios

© The Guidebook Company Ltd

Churubusco Film Studios, which unfortunately tourists are not allowed to visit. In any case, Mexican film technical workers have been staging a work slow-down for several years now, so there is very little shooting to be seen. A few kilometers to the south, on Calle Museo just to the west of Av Division del Norte (nearest public transport is the Xotepingo stop on the light train between Metro Tasqueña and Xochimilco), stands the **Museo Anahuacalli** (free, Tues–Sun, 10 am–2 pm, 3 pm–6 pm), which houses Diego Rivera's archeological collection. This pre-Columbian-motif building, designed in black volcanic stone by Rivera himself, resembles the tomb of some evil totalitarian dictator. Most of the artefacts on display are ceramic figurines and stone sculptures from West and Central Mexican cultures. A two-story atrium contains studies for Rivera's murals and a drawing of a train that he completed at age three. The building stands on a bulge in the lava flow from the Xictli volcano, called the **Pedregal**, which covered the southern suburbs of what is now Mexico City around AD 100.

UNAM AND CUICUILCO

After passing through San Angel, Av Insurgentes enters the **Ciudad Universitaria**, the main campus of the Universidad Nacional Autónoma de México, also known as UNAM. The university, which now has about 300,000 students, was moved here from downtown in 1952. During the 1960s and 1970s, UNAM was a hotbed of political activism, but the current crop of students are definitely more career-oriented (although you do see hippies selling jewelry and left-wing books around the Humanities Building). On the right is the enormous **Mexico 68 Olympic Stadium**, built to resemble either a volcanic cone or a sombrero and with a huge mosaic by Diego Rivera along the exterior. Across Insurgentes begins the vast expanse of the university campus. The 10-story **Library** is decorated with a cryptic mosaic depicting Mexican and European

The scene of Trotsky's assassination, Enrique Diaz

knowledge by Juan O'Gorman, while the nearby **Rectory** has a relief-mosaic by David Alfaro Siquieros that shows the students being egged on by the workers. The campus also houses theaters, museums with temporary exhibitions and sculpture and botanical gardens, but it is best to take wheeled transport to see them, because the distances are great under the hot sun.

South of UNAM, immediately after Insurgentes crosses the Periférico, you reach the ruins of **Cuicuilco** on the left. Around AD 100, this late-Formative site was buried under the Xictli lava flow; it was laboriously excavated during the 1930s. You walk over the lava fields to the main structure, a circular step pyramid 23 meters (75 feet) tall and 118 meters (388 feet) wide. A ramp leads up to the top where there is a two-story deep pit containing an oval stone construction that was probably an altar. A walk around the pyramid's base reveals how deeply the lava buried the site—at least five meters (16 feet). On the southwest side there is an interesting circular group of flat stones leaning inward with red lines painted on the inside; this was possibly also an altar. The small, good **museum** contains many artefacts found on the site, including an incense burner modeled in the shape of the Fire God. West of Cuicuilco across Av Insurgentes, the **1968 Olympic Village** contains a number of other small temples. There are probably many more buried under the lava, but the difficulties of digging through all that rock have impeded investigation.

XOCHIMILCO

About 24 kilometers (15 miles) southeast of the Zócalo lie the floating gardens of Xochimilco ('Place Where Flowers Grow' in Nahuatl). By public transit, the best way to reach here is by *pesero* or *tren ligero* ('light train') from the Tasqueña Metro station;

Mexico City Metro

N

Legend

⊙ Transfer station

0	1	2	3	4	5 kms
0		1		2	3 miles

© Odyssey Publications Ltd

the latter leaves you at the terminus about eight blocks southwest of the center, while the *peseros* stop at the main square. In pre-Hispanic times, this town was a bread-basket of the Valley of Mexico; residents grew huge amounts of flowers and vegetables on *chinampas*, a type of reed-and-mud platform raised out of the shallow lake waters. The Spanish called it the 'Venice of the Americas', but nevertheless burned the town to the ground when the Xochimilcos put up a fierce resistance and almost killed Cortés. The area of cultivation is now greatly reduced due to the draining of the lakes and encroaching urbanization.

Matador and bull, Mexico City

Nevertheless, Xochimilco is a hugely popular weekend excursion for Mexico City residents, who rent flower-bedecked boats to cruise along the polluted canals while eating, drinking and being serenaded by *mariachi* bands floating alongside. You will be approached by many touts who want to take you directly to one of the six *embarcaderos* ('boat docks'); however, there are also sights around the main square. Xochimilco's **market**, whose presence dates back to pre-Hispanic times, is a fine example of a traditional *tianguis* (Nahuatl for 'market'), with some crafts and many house plants grown on *chinampas* for sale. The little **Capilla del Rosario** just west of the market is decorated with Moorish-style tiles that are supposed to look like lace on the façade and gold tiles within. On the east side of the square stands the entrance to the Franciscan **Convento de San Bernardino** (begun 1543), whose façade is one of the best examples of the spare plateresque style. The magnificent single-vaulted nave inside is lined with eight churrigueresque and baroque retables, and the main altar is backed by a baroque retable covered with paintings and sculptures. A large fresco of John the Baptist decorates the wall above the side entrance. The chapel on the right contains a large painting of the Crucifixion. The main landing for Xochimilco's canals, the **Embarcadero de Nativitas**, lies about 1.5 kilometers (one mile) southeast of the convent; there are also smaller landings closer to the center. Nativitas has the most elaborately flower-garlanded boats, an **artisan's market** and numerous restaurants. The boatmen and women are unionized, and the government sets rates for tours and *mariachi* and marimba bands as well as for food and drink. Sundays and holidays are particularly crowded. The Oaxtepec road just east of Xochimilco passes through the Barrio of San Gregorio Atlapulco, known for its ice cream. Stalls along the road sell more varieties than Baskin-Robbins ever dreamed of, including rose, garlic and corn. Eat at your own risk.

¡La Máscara!

Masks were once common in rural Mexico. On a village's saint's day, peasants donned masks and performed in the dances and parades of the fiesta. The masks were made of wood, bone, cloth, and wax and represented tigers, goats, donkeys, bats, lizards, deer, birds, serpents, rabbits, caimans, monkeys, and armadillos. These animalistic images were usually vestiges of pre-Hispanic gods. Death and various demons were also popular. Other masks were based on post-Conquest imagery: La Malinche, the Spanish Swain, Moors and Christians, Black Slaves, Old Men, the Virgin of Guadalupe, Cowboys, and Satan. Community values and history were taught and reinforced through these dances. They were also a welcome entertainment in the village's poverty-stricken existence. The peasants believed that their identities resided in their faces; when they wore a mask, they hid their true soul and were transformed. They became gods and had the power to convert the brutal world of animal spirits they inhabited into one that was fertile and life-giving.

These traditional ways begin to be forgotten when paved roads arrive at a village, bringing with them urban Mexican culture. The natural world recedes, replaced by the pressing demands of television, newspapers, comic books, and Mexico's intrusive government apparatus. Nobody puts on masks at the fiesta anymore, because they have learned that they

continues

Tinieblas (*Darkness*) meets his fans

are already wearing them. The essence of this new life is combat, which in the end they must always lose. Perro Aguayo, one of the great maskless wrestlers, told me: 'Why do I need to wear a mask? I'm already wearing one!' He pointed to his scarred and battered face. Rage, jealousy, treachery and violence are everywhere, and the only way to endure them is to put on a mask of stoicism and resignation every time they step outside their home. 'We are frightened by other people's glances,' says Octavio Paz, 'because the body reveals rather than hides our private selves.' If they take off their masks and open themselves up, all that will be revealed is that they are weak, lonely, crying, and mortal.

With the arrival of the greater urban culture, rural villagers learn that they are impoverished. The only option becomes to move Mexico City in the hope of a better life. In the seventy years since the Mexican revolution, millions have streamed to the capital, leaving women, children, and old people back in their villages. If they are lucky enough to have spare time and spending money, the new city dwellers divert themselves in cavernous, government-owned movie palaces and enormous sports arenas holding tens of thousands. One of these new entertainments was imported from the United States in 1933 by Salvador Lutteroth, a retired revolutionary army colonel; it is *lucha libre* or 'free fighting', the Mexican version of professional wrestling. Through it, real masks—not symbolic ones—have found their way back into Mexican life.

The first *lucha libre* mask was a gimmick, a device used to excite the audience. In 1934, an American wrestler brought the leather mask down from Chicago, and Lutteroth liked the idea. He was dubbed El Enmascarado, 'The Masked Man', and fought a few matches against other Americans in Mexico City (there were only a handful of Mexican wrestlers at this time). This mask provided the model for all those that have followed: form-fitting and covering the entire head. Two years later the promoter decided to bring back masks. Antonio Martinez, a sporting goods retailer, sewed a leather mask for Cyclone McKay, another American, who became El Maravilla Enmascarado. Soon the Masked Marvel was drawing crowds, and the newspapers were calling him 'hated and mysterious'—the mask was a hit. Perhaps a reason for the Masked Marvel's success was that masks were suddenly the rage in Mexico City's popular culture, and Lutteroth was following the trend.

The impulse for this craze came from abroad, the United States and France. In 1936, a New York newspaper published the debut of *The Phantom*, featuring the first great masked and costumed comic strip vigilante. Also known as The Ghost Who Walks, the Phantom wore a skin-tight purple jumpsuit, striped trunks, and a black mask over his eyes. Unlike most later masked heroes (Batman, for example), he almost always wore his mask, even when he was relaxing at home in his skull-shaped cave. In fact, he usually appeared unmasked as a disguise when he was trying to infiltrate some enemy hideout and not tip them off that he was the Phantom. The strip was an instant success and soon sold to newspapers worldwide, including many in Mexico. Suddenly the Mexican public demanded to see wrestlers in masks, and the promoters realized that they were on to a good thing.

Another popular adventure tale in Mexico City of the 1930s was *The Man in the Iron Mask* by Alexandre Dumas. The title character is Philippe, who is the identical twin of Louis XIV of France. The king imprisons his brother in a castle and tortures him until the end of his days by having his head encased in an iron mask that is impossible to remove. When Philippe's true love finds him at the end, the interior of the mask is rusted with his tears. The mask meant pain, and it was unchangeable—that was life in Mexico City. After reading this book, a young wrestler named Rudy Guzmán decided to model his masked character after The Man in the Iron Mask. He became El Santo, El Enmascarado de Plata ('The Saint, The Man in the Silver Mask'), the most famous Mexican wrestler of all time.

Rodolfo Guzmán Huerta moved to Mexico City as a youth and quickly fell in love with *lucha libre*. He trained at the Police Casino gym and in 1939 made his wrestling debut as Rudy Guzmán in one of the city's smaller arenas. He was *rudo*, the Mexican version of the heel or bad guy, and had some impact on the wrestling world but not enough for his ambition. All his friends were donning masks, so he decided to follow suit. His first adopted persona was Murcielago II (The Bat II); this name was a ploy to catch some of the glory of the original Murcielago, the Mexican champion. Unfortunately, Murcielago objected, and Rudy quickly had to drop the idea. A promoter suggested a new name, El Santo; Rudy added 'The Man in the Silver Mask', and a legend was born. Santo's costume was silver, and his mask sported the distinctive teardrop-shaped eyeholes.

continues

El Santo moved quickly to build his name. He switched from the *rudos* camp to the *científicos*, the 'babyfaces' or good guys, who were naturally more popular. He cultivated his reputation out of the ring and became known for being polite, generous, honest, and kind to children. And most important: he never removed his mask. Rene Cardona, the late film director who made dozens of Santo movies, said: 'He was Santo because he never showed his face. He would leave the set with his mask still on. In the studio commissary he ate wearing a mask with a hole for his chin so he could move his jaw.' When a film crew traveled to Miami for a shoot, Santo flew on a different plane so nobody on the production would see his face when

Rayo de Jalisco Junior and Senior pose with Lizmark

he removed his mask for Customs. In his films he even wore his mask when sleeping and when making out with the beautiful female Interpol agents.

Through wrestling, and also films and comic books, Santo became the first Latin American superhero, popular in places as far away as Lebanon. His mask was the equivalent of Superman's 'S'—instantly and universally recognizable. Journalists assured fans that despite his fame, when he walked the streets without his mask he blended with the crowd, just a humble member of Mexico City's millions. When he finally retired in the early 1980s, Santo halted his career by publicly unmasking himself. Underneath he *was* humble; bald, with dark bags under his eyes, he looked like a retired factory worker or craftsman. In 1984 he died of a heart attack, and he lay in state once more masked as in life. Other masked wrestlers attended the wake, tears flowing from their eyeholes. The homely Rodolfo Guzmán Huerta hardly existed; the person buried in the Mausoleo del Angel crypt adorned with a silver bust of the masked hero was El Santo.

In the wake of Santo's success, *lucha libre* began to shed its North American characteristics and become more distinctly Mexican. The mania for masks, which few wrestlers wear in the United States, was just one of the many changes. The conflict in US professional wrestling is usually defined as a fight between the good 'American' wrestler and the wicked, treacherous foreigner. This did not play for very long in Mexico, because the country has not had the same experience of waves of new immigrants arriving and stirring up racist and nativist feelings. In the 1940s, the essential struggle in every *lucha libre* bout was redefined as a battle between *rudo* and *científico*, also known as *técnico*. Santo exemplified the *técnico* side; modest, upstanding, and clean-fighting, he was the pride of the community. The *rudo* was his antithesis. These were the ugly, hairy, and misshapen bullies, mean drunks, and corrupt cops that stalked honest, hardworking citizens and made life hell. *Lucha libre* represented the daily battle on the streets of Mexico City.

As the plot became more Mexican, the characters followed suit. The earliest masked characters were simplistic—Santo's brother donned a black mask and became Black Guzmán—but wrestlers soon realized that they were limited only by the power of their imaginations. Characters began to appear that exemplified the rigors of life in urban Mexico. The white-

continues

masked Medico Asesino ('Assassin Doctor') was a doctor in real life, but in the ring he was a *rudo*, because that's how you survive, by being tough and mean. Within a few decades audiences could see characters tumbling across the ring that represented athletes, animals, professions, religious figures, cowboys, Greek gods, body parts, science, Indians, weather, comic-book characters, and, most prominently, death, horror, and violence.

Another Mexican innovation in the 1940s was the mask-versus-mask match. The promoters saw that the audience loved the mystery of masks; how better to excite them than with a glimpse of what lay below? The rules are simple: the loser of the bout is stripped of his mask and can never wear one again. His face is exposed to the multitudes, and his real name is published throughout the country. The unmasking is a moment of the highest drama; a mythic figure is about to plunge back down to the ranks of the all-too-human. From now on, no matter how threatening and defiant the wrestler is, the audience will always have something on him: his true identity. He is an object of ridicule and humiliation but also of pity. Every Mexico City resident knows that events—from an earthquake to a run-in with a cop—can strip their brave façades in an instant, exposing them, naked and helpless, to the outside world. Wrestlers agree to mask-versus-mask matches because to lose means a big payday. They can lose their mask only once in a career, so they can demand a year's salary or more for one night's work. The winners are given the mask, and every champion wrestler has a trophy room in which opponents' masks hang on the walls like scalps. Masks are also forcibly removed during regular matches to heat up the fans, but this is technically illegal and these mask losses are never permanent. Promoters rarely schedule mask-versus-mask matches because of the expense and to avoid over-exposure of what for the fan is the ultimate moment of *lucha libre*.

The last Mexican transformation of professional wrestling involves the action inside the ring. In the United States, there are rarely more than two people fighting at once, and the fight has a simplistic logic: one move leads inexorably to another, and it is held long enough for the audience to catch the meaning. This is too slow and obvious for Mexican audiences. Most *lucha libre* matches feature two or three wrestlers to a side. They are often in the ring at the same time, hurling themselves off the ropes and at each other in intricate and daring sequences of prearranged moves, resembling an

continues

Super Astro's flying finish

aggressive ballet on fast forward. I asked one American wrestler about *lucha libre*, and he responded, 'That's not wrestling! It doesn't make *sense*.' For Mexican audiences, the speed, complexity, and excitement of the moves overwhelm any need for logic. They have a different taste in storytelling, although the basic plot, the battle between heroes and villains, remains the same.

Lucha libre is now Mexico's second most popular spectator sport after soccer. Any night of the week, it may be seen at one of at least ten arenas across Mexico City, some holding more than 15,000 fans. It has spawned a whole genre of cartoonish adventure movies, dozens of wrestling magazines and the most-watched weekly sports shows. Serious newspapers report the outcome of the previous night's fights, and intellectuals ponder the meaning of professional wrestling in essays and on talk shows. If a Mexican had never seen a *lucha libre* match before, he would at once understand the meaning of the battle unfolding before him. His response to a *rudo*'s obscene gesture at the audience would be automatic—whistles and catcalls. If the concerns of its audience change, *lucha libre* adapts; recently invented *rudo* characters include Texas Ranger and the LA Cops. The sport is so successful because the entire show—characters, masks, moves, obscene gestures, etc—is employed solely to excite and amuse urban Mexico.

Today nearly every young wrestler starts his career masked. Outside the arenas, masked wrestlers appear at awards ceremonies, wrestling movie premières, and at demonstrations called by the National Union of Wrestlers and Referees. The streets in front of Mexico City's many arenas are filled with vendors selling posters, masks, dolls, and miniature wrestling rings. Child-sized wrestling masks are the most popular gifts on Three Kings Day, when Mexican children receive their holiday presents. The symbol of the Asamblea de Barrios, a grass-roots movement to defend Mexico's poor neighborhoods, is an overweight wrestler named Superbarrio. He leads marches, disrupts the Mexican Congress, and has become a respected national figure of the left-wing opposition. Masked wrestlers are even showing up in the paintings of major avant-garde artists. The popularity of the wrestling mask has led to grumbling by some veteran wrestlers who owe their careers to their masks. They fear that the mask has been debased, that there is no mystery left. Huaracán Ramírez told me, 'It's *máscaritis*—a disease!'

Ancient Olmec colossal head and modern Mexico City

CABEZA COLOSAL N 1 DESCUBIERTA EN EL PUEBLO
DE SAN LORENZO TENOCHTITLAN EDO. DE VER POR
MATTHEW S. STERLING. CIVILIZACION OLMECA (1200 A 900 A C)

Around Mexico City

Introduction

Since the ascendancy of the Aztecs, the states surrounding Mexico City have either been in thrall to the capital or at war with it. Today many of them are in danger of becoming mere suburbs, as Mexico City spreads its octopus-like tentacles in all directions. Before the Aztec era, the Olmecs, Teotihuacanos, Mayas and Toltecs all built major cities here, and some of their monuments, like the pyramids in Teotihuacán, are wonders of the world. This area was also the center of colonial development and contains many of the most elaborate churches in Mexico. Despite the region's heavy urbanization, there are still many opportunities to escape into the natural world, like in the gardens of Morelos and the park between the immense volcanoes of Popocatépetl and Iztaccíhuatl.

The state of Mexico, popularly called **Edomex** (short for *Estado de México*), includes Teotihuacán, the most renowned and unforgettable archeological site in Mexico. This vast ruined city, which is bisected by the Avenue of the Dead, contains the enormous Pyramids of the Sun and Moon and numerous palaces decorated with newly discovered murals. In the heart of the traditional town of Tepotzotlán stands one of the most ornate baroque churches in Mexico; the gilt churrigueresque décor is at times a meter thick. The convent next door houses the finest collection of religious art in Mexico. Just over the border of the state of Hidalgo, the archeological site of Tula, with its huge stone warrior-columns, called 'Atlantes', provides a fascinating glimpse into the warlike Toltec civilization. Edomex's capital, the industrial city of Toluca, attracts thousands of Indian craftsmen to its famous Friday market. To the south of Toluca, the archeological site of Malinalco, situated above a charming traditional village of the same name, contains a unique circular Aztec temple dedicated to eagle and jaguar warriors carved from the solid rock of the hillside.

The mild climate of the state of Morelos has made it a popular vacation spot since Aztec times. Cuernavaca, the capital, is still the favorite weekend destination of Mexico City's wealthy and powerful. Among its sights are a pyramid, Cortés' palace, beautiful gardens, many artisan markets and a huge, old cathedral. In the countryside you can find fascinating but infrequently visited archeological sites like Tepoztlán—above the town of the same name famous for its crafts market—and Xochicalco. The latter was a sprawling fortified city that covered a hillside; at the summit stands the Temple of the Feathered Serpent, whose stone reliefs are in a remarkable state of preservation. The city of Taxco just over the border in the state of Guerrero is a colonial jewel. Its cobblestone streets, red-tile-roofed houses and fantastically ornate Santa

Prisca church were originally built by silver barons. Today Taxco is home to an industry devoted to the manufacture and sale of high quality silver jewelry—a bargain-hunter's dream.

The state of Puebla was long the second most important region in Mexico after the capital. Now somewhat eclipsed by the industrial north, it is still home to some of the finest colonial architecture in Mexico. The center of Puebla, the capital, is filled with churches and mansions covered with the distinctive local tiles. The cathedral is a colonial masterpiece, and the Capilla del Rosario in the church of Santo Domingo is lined with remarkable gilt carvings covering every square inch of the interior. The newly opened Museo Amparo houses an excellent collection of pre-Columbian art from Central Mexico. Puebla is also known for its culinary specialties, particularly the spicy *mole a la poblana* sauce and *camotes*, a delicious local candy made from sweet potatoes. Cholula, on the western outskirts of Puebla, was an important Indian sacred center and contains the as-yet-unexcavated Great Pyramid, the most massive structure in the New World. Nearby are the stunning churches of Tonanzintla and Acatepec.

Tlaxcala, the smallest state in Mexico, is home to the pre-Hispanic murals of Cacaxtla, the best preserved and most lurid in all Mexico. The state capital, also with the same name, contains a remarkable early convent and, on a hill above town, the confection-like church of Ocotlán, one of the great masterpieces of the churrigueresque.

Getting There

Almost all the sights in the state of Mexico lie within two hours of downtown Mexico City—even with traffic jams. To reach the great pyramids of Teotihuacán, take Mexico 85 (the Pachuca toll road) north and turn east at the Teotihuacán exit, from which it is another 25 kilometers (16 miles). Buses for the ruins leave frequently from the Indios Verdes Metro station and also from the Terminal Norte bus station. The baroque monastery of Tepotzotlán stands a few kilometers west of the Mexico 57 to Querétaro; the exit is 42 kilometers (26 miles) north of downtown Mexico City. By public transport, you can reach this town either by bus from a station three blocks east of Metro Tacuba or via *combi* from Metro Cuatro Caminos. The Toltec site of Tula, across the border in the state of Hidalgo, lies just east of the town of Tula de Allende; 15 kilometers (nine miles) north of Tepotzotlán exit from Mexico 57 and then drive east 18 kilometers (11 miles). Toluca, famous for its market, lies due west of the capital on Mexico 15, 67 kilometers (42 miles) from the Zócalo. Many buses and (slower) trains also run this route. Malinalco, with a pyramid carved of solid

*Jade mask,
Anthropology Museum*

rock, is ten kilometers (six miles) east of Tenancingo on Mexico 55 between Toluca and Taxco. The pilgrimage site of Chalma lies a few kilometers further east. The great volcanoes of Popocatépetl and Iztaccíhuatl stand east of Mexico City and may be reached from Amecameca or via a rough dirt road (two to three hours in good conditions) from Cholula in Puebla.

The state of Morelos lies just over the mountains south of Mexico City. Cuernavaca is 53 kilometers (33 miles) south of the capital on Mexico 95, a scenic toll road. Dozens of buses run here daily from the Central Camionera del Sur. The site of Tepoztlán lies 26 kilometers (16 miles) east of Cuernavaca, while the ruins of Xochicalco stand a few kilometers east of the Mexico 95 exit, 25 kilometers (15.5 miles) south of the city. Mexico 95 continues south to the state of Guerrero and the turnoff for the silver city of Taxco is just south of the border. The Olmec carvings of Chalcatzingo are found near the town of Jonacatepec, off Mexico 160 and 20 kilometers (12 miles) southeast of Cuautla.

The state of Puebla extends east of the huge volcanoes on the Valley of Mexico's eastern edge. Mexico 150 heads over the pine-forest-covered ridge 112 kilometers (70 miles) to Puebla, the state capital. Puebla's airport has regular flights to Tijuana and Guadalajara. Buses run here every 15 minutes from Mexico City's Central Camionera del Oriente. Trains to Puebla from the capital are very slow and continue either to Jalapa and Veracruz or southeast to Oaxaca. The ruins of Cholula lie about ten kilometers (six miles) east of Puebla; there are frequent mini-buses that ply the route.

The tiny state of Tlaxcala begins just north of Puebla's outskirts. The state capital, Tlaxcala, lies 33 kilometers (20 miles) from the city of Puebla. The Maya murals of Cacaxtla are southwest of Tlaxcala, halfway to San Martin Texmelucán in Puebla. The easiest way to reach them is via the Puebla–Tlaxcala highway; the turn-off is to the left a few kilometers after you enter Tlaxcala. There is also is an exit for Cacaxtla off the Tlaxcala–San Martin Texmelucán free highway; the ruins are about ten kilometers (six miles) east. Look for the huge hangar-like structure in the hills.

State of Mexico

The state of Mexico rings the Valley of Mexico outside of Mexico City and also bulges far to the southwest almost to the Río Balsas. The Valley of Mexico has been occupied for many millennia. In the town of Santa Isabel Iztapán just north of Mexico City, ditch diggers found the remains of two mammoths that had been butchered with stone and obsidian knives around 12,000–10,000 BC. Closer to our era, settlements show the influence of the Olmec culture from the Gulf coast. Just after the birth of Christ, a plan for a city was laid out in the northeastern corner of the Valley of Mexico. No one knows where the builders came from, but the city became Teotihuacán, the most powerful urban center in Mesoamerica for seven centuries. The enormous Pyramids of the Sun and Moon are two of the marvels of the world. At its height in AD 600, Teotihuacán contained 200,000 people, making it the sixth largest city in the world at the time. Teotihuacán probably sustained itself through trade; the city contained wards for Zapotecs, Mayas and other tribes, and artefacts made here have been found as far away as Guatemala. Around AD 700 unknown tribes invaded and burned the city. The Toltecs and later the Aztecs made pilgrimages to Teotihuacán, because they believed the gods resided in the huge pyramids. The Toltecs controlled the Valley of Mexico from Tula, while the Otomis to the west had capitals in Toluca and Malinalco.

After the Toltec collapse, their descendants mingled with the Otomis and Chichimecs from the north to become a new Toltec-Chichimec culture centered around the valley's network of lakes. The major settlements included Chalco and Texcoco, which was ruled by a family of philosopher-kings. By 1427, these tribes had been subjugated by a savage tribe of Chichimecs who called themselves the Mexica and had recently moved to Tenochtitlán, an island in the middle of the lakes. They founded the Aztec empire that ruled central Mexico for almost a century. When Bernal Díaz del Castillo entered the valley with Cortés, the marvelous scene before him led him to write: 'With such wondrous sights to gaze on we did not know what to say, or if this was real that we saw before our eyes.' After

Teotihuacán sculpture: the God of Death

the Conquest in 1521, Cortés and his captains divided the Valley of Mexico into *encomiendas*, large estates (Cortés took the largest). Mexico City became the Spanish capital and development quickly extended throughout the valley. Indian culture disappeared under the onslaught of Franciscan and Dominican missionaries, new forms of agriculture, early industries, mines and epidemics.

In November 1810, hope of a speedy finish to Mexico's battle for independence ended when Miguel Hidalgo halted his army in a pass between Toluca and Mexico City and decided to return north rather than attack the capital. Over the next decade Toluca was the site of many battles between Morelos' army and the Royalists. In 1910, Zapata's peasant revolutionary army entered the state from the south and within two years controlled Chalco and Amecameca on Mexico City's outskirts. Through much of the Revolution, hunger, disease and looting were rampant in the region. Over the last forty years Mexico City has expanded its boundaries and transformed what once were quiet towns and farming villages into heavily polluted suburbs. Only the mountainous west and southwest of the state remain predominately rural.

TEOTIHUACÁN

The ancient city of Teotihuacán lies in the northeasternmost extension of the valley of Mexico and is so massive that it itself looks like a geological formation. A ring road circumnavigates the site, which archeologists believe covered at least 20 square kilometers. Access to the ruins is through one of three principal entrances. The east entrance is nearest the museum and the Pyramid of the Sun. The Temple of Quetzal-coatl stands a short walk away from the southwest entrance, while the northwest entrance is closest to the Pyramid of the Moon. Admission is charged every time you enter the grounds, so it is expensive to visit one end of the city and then drive over to the next. To see everything inexpensively, you must be prepared to walk. Arrive early, because the sun is intense—hats are a must—and beware of afternoon thunderstorms during the summer months.

Teotihuacán is bisected by the **Avenue of the Dead**, which begins at the Pyramid of the Moon, passes the Citadel three kilometers (two miles) to the south and, although this part hasn't been reconstructed, continues for another two miles. The city plan is oriented a little east of due north; archeologists believe that this alignment had astronomical significance. If you enter the site at the south entrance (whose parking lot may have been the city's main market), the first building that faces you across the Avenue of the Dead is the **Citadel**, so called because this walled enclosure resembles a fortress. Thirteen small temples stand along the Citadel's walls. Within this enclosure is the **Temple of Quetzalcoatl**, a low pyramid with six tiers. Each tier is decorated with alternating stone heads of the Feathered Serpent and the Fire Serpent, perhaps representing a mythic moment of creation. The pyramid was originally brightly painted and traces of a blue background may still be seen.

Teotihuacán

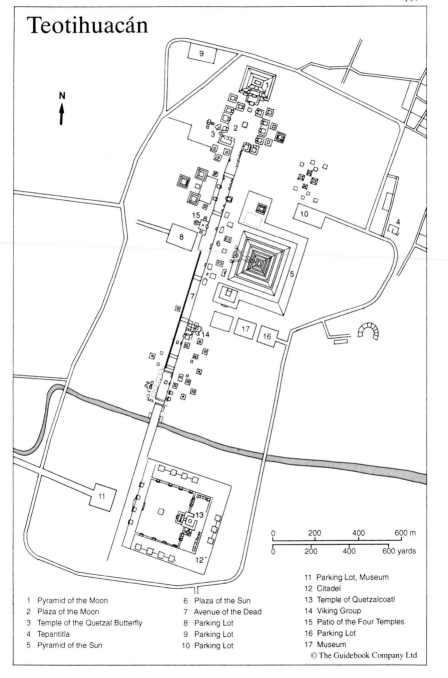

1 Pyramid of the Moon
2 Plaza of the Moon
3 Temple of the Quetzal Butterfly
4 Tepantitla
5 Pyramid of the Sun

6 Plaza of the Sun
7 Avenue of the Dead
8 Parking Lot
9 Parking Lot
10 Parking Lot

11 Parking Lot, Museum
12 Citadel
13 Temple of Quetzalcoatl
14 Viking Group
15 Patio of the Four Temples
16 Parking Lot
17 Museum

© The Guidebook Company Ltd

Returning to the Avenue of the Dead and heading north, you will see on either side remains of building complexes that probably were palaces. The ordinary citizens lived away from the avenue in densely packed complexes of apartments and court-yards. Archeologists believe that Teotihuacán developed through intensive trade rather than agriculture, and wards of the city were reserved for different tribes, in-cluding Mayas and Zapotecs. After a long walk you come to the **Pyramid of the Sun** looming to the right. Seventy meters (230 feet) tall, 225 meters (740 feet) to a side at the base, and containing 1,175,000 cubic meters (4,150,000 cubic feet) of rubble fill, this pyramid is one of the wonders of the world. It was probably built around AD 100, a century or so before the Pyramid of the Moon. In the front is a plaza that was probably a ceremonial space. Archeologists believe Teotihuacán's pyramids were not funerary monuments like the pyramids of Egypt. In 1971, they discovered a lava tube beneath the Pyramid of the Sun that had been artificially widened and ended in a chamber. This may have been the most important religious site in Teotihuacán, a kind of womb for the gods. At 2,300 meters (7,565 feet), the climb to the top of the Pyramid of the Sun literally takes your breath away, so go slowly. The view is defi-nitely worth it.

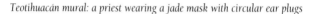

Teotihuacán mural: a priest wearing a jade mask with circular ear plugs

Just south of the Pyramid of the Sun lies the new **museum**. This semi-sunken glass structure is topped with thick greenery, giving it a Hanging Gardens Of Babylon look. Inside you will find excellent exhibitions devoted to Teotihuacan's history, environment, religion and social organization, including some fine objects found during recent excavations. The most dramatic room contains a diorama of the site under a glass floor and a magnificent view of the Pyramid of the Moon through a gigantic window.

Northeast of the pyramid, an entrance to the east of the ringroad takes you to Tepantitla, one of ancient Teotihuacan's many residential quarters. This contains the famous *Paradise of Tlaloc* mural that archeologists now believe represents not the rain god but the Great Goddess, one of Teotihuacan's principal deities. The **Pyramid of the Moon** at the north end of the Avenue of the Dead is smaller and steeper, with a fine view down the avenue. All the major buildings in Teotihuacán were covered with plaster and painted, usually red; they must have made quite a sight at sunset. On the west side of the plaza in front of the Pyramid of the Moon stands the **Palace of the Quetzal Butterfly**; the patio is surrounded with carvings of birds and butterflies and remnants of geometric murals. A few steps to the west lies the **Palace of the Jaguars**, a sunken residential complex containing murals of plumed feline blowing conch shells. The building complexes lying along the Avenue of the Dead to the south also contain many fragments of murals. The restaurants outside the site entrances are generally expensive; for cheaper food try the nearby town of San Juan Teotihuacán.

The **Augustinian convent** (1560) at Acolman, a few kilometers south of Teotihuacán on the free road, makes an interesting stop on your return to the city. This enormous church/convent complex is now being restored to its former glory. The church's façade is one of the finest in the simple plateresque style; and just to the right is the **open chapel**, built to hold the crowds of Indian converts who could not fit in the church. Inside are murals depicting famous Augustinian friars and gilt baroque retables. The convent's cloister is decorated with 16th-century frescoes and has a grove of orange trees in the courtyard.

TEPOTZOTLÁN

Forty-two kilometers (twenty-six miles) north of the city, Tepotzotlán used to be a country town, a favorite Sunday retreat for city residents. Go there soon, because an industrial corridor is creeping north up the Querétaro highway and will probably engulf this town within five years. Tepotzotlán's great jewel, right on the main square, is the **Colegio de San Francisco Javier**, founded in 1582 by Jesuits and one of Mexico's foremost schools until the order's expulsion in 1767. This is one of the masterpieces of the churrigueresque; no expense was spared as detail was piled on

Three Aztec Myths

Aztlán

Tenochtitlán was founded by a tribe whose origins lay far away to the northwest, in Aztlán ('Place of Whiteness' or 'Place of Herons'). Aztlán was an island in the middle of a lake, and its inhabitants called themselves the Aztecs. They were simple fishermen who lived off the lake's abundant fish and game. Their god was Huitzilopochtli ('Hummingbird on the left'); he may have originally been the tribe's chieftain. One day Huitzilopochtli commanded the Aztecs to leave their home, promising them vast riches and the conquest of all the peoples of the universe. Clad in animal skins and bearing a few simple possessions, they embarked on their exodus shortly after AD 1100. Their first stop was the rock called Chicomoztoc, or 'Seven Caves', after the tunnels that penetrated the hill. This was a time of trial; Chicomoztoc was surrounded by fierce beasts and thorny bushes. When they finally emerged from the caves, they had a new name, the Mexica, and they carried bows and arrows. They wandered to the southeast, led by Huitzilopochtli who whispered commands to four priest-rulers carrying his idol on their shoulders. Next they reached Culhuacán ('Curved Mountain'), where Huitzilopochtli's sister, the sorceress Malinalxochitl, tried to challenge her brother's ascendancy with spells and threats. In the middle of the night, the god woke his followers and bade them move on while his sister slept. Huitzilopochtli would not always be so lenient with treachery. The next morning, Malinalxochitl awoke to her abandonment; she and her supporters later moved south to found Malinalco. The Mexica wandered across northern Mexico for years. They would stay in one place for a few seasons, planting corn, building courts for the ball game and sacrificing people to Huitzilopochtli. Then they would move on, impelled as always by the demands of their god. Fifty-two years after leaving Chicomoztoc, the Mexica arrived at the hill of Coatepec near Tula, where their god would be reborn. Today, the exodus from Aztlán is re-enacted hundreds of times daily as Mexican peasants leave poor rural communities to seek their fortunes in Mexico City.

QUETZALCOATL

There were two Quetzalcoatls: one was a god, the Feathered Serpent, associated with the wind; the other was Topiltzin Quetzalcoatl, the king of Tula, who took on some of his namesake's characteristics. His story became one of the dominant myths, not just of the Aztecs but of almost all Mesoamerican cultures during the late Post-Classic era. The king Quetzalcoatl lived in a tall temple in the heart of Tula. He hid his bearded face behind a cloth, because it was monstrous, like a battered rock. His temple was surrounded by four buildings pointing to the four directions; each was covered with precious materials—jade, gold, shells and turquoise. From Quetzalcoatl all culture flowed; he invented the calendar and taught the Tulans goldworking, stonecarving and making fabrics from feathers. There was no poverty or hunger. The crops were huge—you could barely grasp an ear of corn in your arms, and the amaranth plants grew as tall as palm trees—and the cotton grew colored in all the hues of the rainbow. In Tula lived all the birds with precious feathers, including the quetzal and the roseate spoonbill, and each tried to outdo the other with its song. When Tezcatlipoca ('Smoking Mirror'), the terrible god of sorcerers and warriors, saw that the Tulans had forgotten him due to Quetzalcoatl's benevolence, he became jealous. He disguised himself as a sorcerer and went among the Tulans. He tried to convince them to begin human sacrifice again, but Quetzalcoatl refused because he loved his people. One day Tezcatlipoca approached the king, who was old and sick, with a gourd full of *pulque*, an alcoholic drink made from maguey juice. 'This gourd contains medicine that will make you better,' said the sorcerer. 'Drink it.' Quetzalcoatl refused again and again, until finally the sorcerer convinced him to take a little sip. 'It tastes good,' said the king, who then took a big drink. Quetzalcoatl was soon drunk, and in that state he slept with his sister, because he did not know her. The next morning, the king was so ashamed that he decided to abandon Tula. He burned his palaces and buried his riches and set out for the east. Tezcatlipoca's followers, ruthless warriors, took over Tula and began human

continues

sacrifice again. When Quetzalcoatl reached the Gulf of Mexico, some say that he embarked on a raft of serpents and disappeared over the horizon. Others say that he burned himself on a pyre and his spirit rose up to become the Morning Star. Five centuries later, Quetzalcoatl's memory weighed heavily on the Aztec emperor Motecuhzoma II, who wavered between allegiance to the ruthless warriors and a more benevolent system of government. When he heard that bearded men had landed on his shores, he speculated that this was Quetzalcoatl returned from the east. By the time he realized his error, it was too late.

THE LEGEND OF COYOLXAUHQUI

On top of Coatepec ('Hill of the Serpent') lived a woman named Coatlicue, or 'She of the Serpent Skirt'. She was the mother of the 400 gods and of their sister Coyolxauhqui. Coatlicue's sacred chore was to sweep the hill, and one day while she was sweeping a ball of feathers fell on her. She put the feathers in her bosom and continued sweeping. After she had finished, she looked for them and they were gone. She was pregnant at that moment. When her 400 sons learned of her state, they became furious at her for dishonoring them. 'We must kill her,' said her daughter, Coyolxauhqui. When Coatlicue heard

Coatlicue, the Earth Goddess, Anthropology Museum

this, she was very frightened. However, the child in her womb was Huitzilopochtli and he told her not to be afraid. One of the 400 sons turned traitor on his brothers and told Huitzilopochtli that they were putting on their war gear and preparing to kill him. Coyolxauhqui led the charge of the 400 up the hill of Coatepec. She cut off her mother's head, and two snakes sprang out of the neck in its place. At that moment Huitzilopochtli was born, fully garbed for battle with his face painted blue and carrying a shield and weapons. His most potent armament was a flaming serpent, with which he struck off Coyolxauhqui's head. Her body rolled down the hill and broke into many pieces. Huitzilopochtli chased his 400 brothers down Coatepec and kept at their heels as they ran four times around the base of the hill. Although they begged for mercy, he slew almost all of them; the few that escaped fled to the south and became the gods of that quarter. Huitzilopochtli stripped the bodies and put on their armor, making their insignia his own. In celebration, he ordered the damming of a river that flowed by Coatepec. The new lake filled with fish and game, and the Aztecs relived the bounty of Aztlán, a bounty that foreshadowed their future capital in Tenochtitlán. When Huitzilopochtli ordered the tribe to move on, some wanted to remain and enjoy the largesse. The god became furious, destroyed the dam and killed the malingerers. The rest of the tribe headed to Tula, where they paid tribute to the glories of the Toltec empire and its king, Quetzalcoatl. Then they marched into the Valley of Mexico, where they fulfilled the prophecies of their reborn god. After they founded Tenochtitlán, their priest-rulers told the Mexica that they must sacrifice great numbers of prisoners-of-war, in order that Huitzilo-pochtli might win the battle with his brothers and sister that was re-enacted every night. Huitzilopochtli was the sun, and his siblings were associated with the night. If he did not have enough hearts and blood to fuel his strength, day would never come and the universe would collapse.

detail until the whole was a teeming mass of ornament. The décor of the church's single tower (begun in 1670) is so profuse that it appears organic; backlit, it can look like a mountain from a Chinese brush painting. Four rows of *estípites* run up the façade; between are cameo sculptures of saints. The 16th-century **monastery** to the left is now the **Museo Nacional del Virreynato** (Wed–Sun, 11 am–5.30 pm; Tues half the rooms open), a treasure trove of colonial religious art. The first floor walkway around the cloister is decorated with scenes from the life of San Ignacio Loyola, founder of the Jesuit order. Exhibitions on the first floor tell the tale of the Conquest and colonization through some remarkable objects, including ivory carvings from the Far East. The **Presbytery**, or Domestic Chapel, was reserved for novices. Mirrors cover its unique churrigueresque altar, which displays the image of the Virgen del Rosario. To the left is a statue of the wealthy aristocrat who donated the chapel. The highlight of this complex is the interior of the **Iglesia de San Francisco Javier**, whose façade was admired earlier. This is one of the three greatest churrigueresque interiors in Mexico (the others are in Taxco and Tlaxcala). It is so filled with ornament, at times a meter deep, that the building's structure is invisible and the retables seem about to whirl into motion. An entrance in the left wall takes you to the **Capilla de la Virgen de Loreto**. This little house, which almost fills the room, is a replica of the Virgin Mary's home. According to legend, it flew away from Palestine on the arrival of the Muslims and eventually landed in the Italian town of Loreto. You can peer through the windows and see a small altar and other décor in a poor state of repair.

The **Camarín** behind the house is a tiny octagonal room covered with gold ornament and sculptures of archangels, cherubim and black slaves holding baskets. Up in the miniscule dome, the Holy Ghost, saints and more cherubim stare down at you. To one side of the Capilla de Loreto, the **Relicario de San José** is a small room, once again covered with gold ornament, and housing a small but tremendously detailed gilt altar. Returning to the monastery museum, more paintings and sculpture are displayed on the second floor. Particularly interesting are the portraits of pious nuns dressed as the Bride of Christ. A balcony has a good view of the lush valley. The monastery's basement is devoted to more practical pursuits, like the kitchen, wine cellar and the entrance to the spacious gardens. The **Parrocco** just to the left of the monastery entrance is the town church, with a stern façade and a baroque altar inside.

Also attached to the complex is the **Hostería del Convento**, an excellent traditional restaurant in a beautiful setting. Other restaurants are found on the square, but they pale in comparison. Before Christmas, Tepotzotlán holds a famous **Passion Play** that attracts tens of thousands. You need tickets; a number of Mexico City tour operators offer packages that give you tickets, transport and a meal.

Ancient volcanic crater in Nevada de Toluca National Park, State of Mexico

TOLUCA

The state of Mexico's capital, the industrial city of **Toluca** (pop 600,000), lies in a plain west of the Valley of Mexico's ring of mountains. Most tourists come here for its **Friday market**, housed in a vast prefabricated shed on the southeast perimeter of Paseo Tollocan, the city's ring road. Thousands of Indian artisans from the surrounding villages and the state of Michoacán come to the market next to the central bus station to sell their crafts, including baskets, pottery and textiles. The preliminary prices are usually excessive, so bargain hard. The market is open the rest of the week as well, but the selection is smaller. More mundane articles, like plastic buckets, shoes, fruit, prepared food and so on, are also available. Watch for pickpockets and don't get lost—the market is vast.

At the **Casa de los Artesanías**, also known as Casart, on Paseo Tollocan 700 a few blocks east, you can buy reasonably priced crafts in a less hectic setting. Mainly stocking ceramics, the store's quality is not as high as you find in Mexico City. Toluca is not exactly a beauty spot, but there are other worthwhile sights, mostly grouped around the **Plaza Fray Andrés de Castro** in the north center of town. Encompassing about four city blocks, this square is ringed by portals and contains the principal government buildings and the new Cathedral. Stores under the portals sell *moscos*, a locally produced orange liqueur, and beautiful religious candles. One block north, the **Cosmo Vitral** is a greenhouse complex whose walls are art nouveau-style stained glass.

MALINALCO AND CHALMA

The archeological site of Malinalco stands on a ledge on the steep hillside above the town of the same name, which lies 11 kilometers (seven miles) east of Tenancingo (48 kilometers, 30 miles south of Toluca). Houses in this little town are covered with traditional red-tile roofs; its **Augustinian convent** in the plaza is also worth visiting. A road leads from the plaza about half a kilometer (0.3 miles) up to the hillside, where you find the **site entrance** and a small **museum** reconstructing the ruins. From here you take a path that zig-zags up the hill for about 20 minutes until you arrive at the ruins.

The Aztecs conquered this area during the 15th century and constructed Malinalco between AD 1501 and 1515. The first building is the amazing **Temple I**, a circular structure carved out of the yellow rock of the hillside. It is topped with a thatched roof that protects it from the elements but probably also replicates its original covering. Sculptures of jaguars guard the base of the staircase leading up to the sanctuary, and on top you find two large snake sculptures. The rock around the entrance has been carved in the form of a giant serpent's face, as if you were entering its mouth (these often symbolized caves). The circular room inside is adorned with sculptures of eagles and jaguars rising out of the rock floor. This temple was built as a holy place for Eagle and Jaguar Knights, the two great Aztec warrior orders. Beyond Temple I are more structures, built from stone block, one of which is another circular room. More foundations are visible further along the hillside and in the valley below.

The tiny town of **Chalma** east of Malinalco was a pilgrimage destination during pre-Hispanic times, when Indians worshipped the god Tezcatlipoca ('Smoking Mirror') in a cave here. In 1539, two years after the arrival of Augustinian fathers, the image of **Santo Cristo de Chalma** miraculously appeared in the same cave. The image was moved to a chapel in 1550 and the church was begun in the 17th century. Chalma is one of the most popular pilgrimage spots in Mexico and attracts huge crowds on Sundays and religious holidays. In 1991, almost 50 of the faithful died in a panicked crowd unable to exit the church with so many entering. Chalma lies in a little valley and is reached by a terrible road that loops up over a hill, past some grubby hotels and huge dirt parking lots, and then turns down again. The sanctuary sits beside the stream at the bottom of the hill. To reach it, you head down one of a number of pedestrian-only streets—all claiming to be the 'short way'—lined with an incredible profusion of vendors. Here you can buy souvenir candy, paintings, medallions, crucifixes, 'Memory of Chalma' mugs and snacks. All paths end up at the sanctuary courtyard. It is usually filled with pilgrims, many carrying knapsacks or bed rolls and covered with dust. Some look like wandering holy men, with matted hair and well-worn wooden staffs in their hands. They have hiked here all the way from Mexico City or further. On arrival they put on crowns of roses and other flowers and have their picture taken. To the right of the courtyard is a three-story hostel with simple beds and medical services for the pilgrims, many of whom are limping.

The impressive **sanctuary interior** is all gold gilt and white, with huge Corinthian columns. The venerated Christ of Chalma icon is housed in a gold case, which you can climb behind to kiss the glass and drop coins into the collection box. Behind the altar is a room with huge paintings depicting the story of the image's appearance in a cave. Here teams of priests bless pilgrims with holy water and hear confessions. Further into the complex you find the 'official' Chalma souvenir stand and a hospital. After visiting the sanctuary, pilgrims soak their feet or swim in the stream.

IZTACCÍHUATL AND POPOCATÉPETL

On Mexico City's rare clear days (and early on some not-so-clear mornings) the twin volcanoes of Iztaccíhuatl ('The White Lady') and Popocatépetl ('Smoking Mountain') loom over the eastern skyline. 'Popo' at 5,465 meters (17,976 feet) is slightly higher than Iztaccíhuatl (5,230 meters, 17,203 feet) to the north. Popocatépetl has recently become more active; occasional eruptions and a constant plume of smoke have spread ashes on, depending on which way the wind is blowing, either the Valley of Mexico or Puebla. The view from airplanes traveling between Mexico City and Yucatan is sometimes spectacular. Many of the towns on the east side of the volcano have been abandoned, and visitors are occasionally banned from the volcano's western slopes. They are reached from the charming, traditional town of **Amecameca**, which is also known for the **Capilla del Señor del Sacro Monte**, one of Mexico's most venerated images, on the little hill next to town.

A road heading east from Amecameca winds up to the **Paso de Cortés** ('Cortés' Pass') in the saddle between the mountains. Indian vendors line the roadside selling snacks and milky *pulque*, the potent Aztec drink made from fermented maguey juice. Cortés' army marched through the *paso* on their way to Tenochtitlán in 1519. A road to the right leads up Popocatépetl to **Tlamacas**, a tiny settlement with a hostel for hikers and mountain climbers getting acclimatized to the altitude. The ascent of this volcano should only be attempted by experienced climbers with crampons and ice axes. The ascent of Iztaccíhuatl is slightly less difficult; the path begins at the microwave tower parking lot, 12 kilometers (7.5 miles) along a dirt road north of the Paso de Cortés.

On the other side of the *paso*, there are a handful of small resort hotels in the forest. From here you can take a dirt road (now closed due to eruptions) all the way

*Iztaccíhuatl and Popocatépetl,
Mexico City's nearby volcanoes*

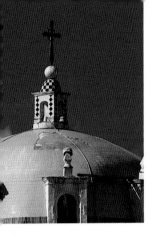

to the town of Cholula in the state of Puebla. The trip takes two to three hours, but you must have a rugged vehicle, at least a VW Beetle, and it is not advisable in wet weather. The forested landscape and views of the volcanoes are stunning, and the road passes through some little towns whose life looks unchanged since the 19th century. Due to Popo's increased activity—it's ash has even reached Mexico City—the authorities may place may place the area around the volcano on a yellow or red alert, closing all hiking trails and severely curtailing tourist activity.

State of Hidalgo

After the decline of Teotihuacán, a chief named Mixcoatl ('Cloud Serpent') led his tribe into the state of Hidalgo from the northwest. They were called the Toltecs, and Mixcoatl's son, the bearded and pale-skinned Topiltzin, founded their capital in Tula in southern Hidalgo around AD 950. The city was soon torn by conflict between those who worshipped the peaceful Feathered Serpent, including Topiltzin, and those who followed the blood-thirsty god Tezcatlipoca ('Smoking Mirror'). Topiltzin was expelled from Tula around AD 987, and his subsequent wanderings south and east became the stuff of myth. According to one tale, he set sail in a raft from the Gulf coast vowing one day to return (Motecuhzoma II remembered this story with fear when he heard of bearded white men landing on his shores.) With the warrior faction in power, the Toltecs extended their influence throughout Central Mexico from Zacatecas to Oaxaca. The Aztecs later looked back on the Toltec era as a time of unparalleled prosperity. Tula collapsed due to internal strife in the mid-12th century, and the survivors streamed forth to conquer and settle lands as far away as Yucatán. Cortés entered Hidalgo in 1520 but was not able to conquer the tribes there completely until 1530.

Tula

The archeological site of Tula, once the capital of the warlike Toltec empire, sits on a hilltop east of Tula de Allende, a dusty town whose bustle is prompted by a nearby Pemex refinery. Unfortunately for visitors, some of Tula's great sculptures, like the warrior-pillars, have been removed and replaced by copies. You can see them in the Anthropological Museum in Mexico City. The **museum** at the site entrance has an excellent exhibition on Tula's history and examples of Toltec pottery and stone work. A gift shop and a café are also on the premises. The city covered 14 square kilometers (5.4 square miles) at its height and probably had a population of 30,000–40,000. Foundations of a residential district can be seen immediately after passing through the entrance complex.

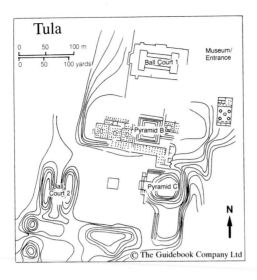

The main ruins lie 600 meters (half a mile) down a walkway lined with little signs exhorting you to 'Walk, Observe and Enjoy!' (and they could add, wear a hat!) The path takes you to **Ball Court No 1** on the right, whose design the Toltecs apparently copied from one at Xochicalco in Morelos. On the left stands the four-tiered **Pyramid B**, the most impressive structure on the site. A wall that runs along the pyramid's north side holds a 40-meter (131-foot) mural called the *Serpent Wall*, which depicts snakes eating human skeletons. Rows of square pillars abut the west side of the pyramid; these were probably meeting halls with muraled walls. More pillars range in front of the pyramid's staircase; these originally held reliefs of marching warriors and held up the roof of an entrance hall. Among the columns lie two *chac mool*, reclining stone figures with a dish in the mid-section that probably received human hearts. The sides of the pyramid are covered with reliefs symbolically depicting the main Toltec warrior orders: jaguars, coyotes, eagles eating hearts and monster-like faces that may be Quetzalcóatl. The platform on top of the pyramid held a temple with two rooms. The wooden roof of the first room was held up by four 'Atlantes' (Atlas-like figures); these are 4.6-meter (15-foot) tall stone columns carved in the shape of Toltec warriors holding an *atlatl* (a stick for hurling arrows) in one hand and a copal incense pouch in the other. The warriors' chests are covered with stylized butterflies, the symbol of the Toltecs. Four square stone columns carved with warrior symbols held up the roof of the rear room, which was the site of the most important altar. The plaza south of Pyramid B has a small ceremonial platform in the center and the remains of **Pyramid C**. Only partially excavated, the latter was the largest structure in Tula. Another ball court lies west across the plaza.

Crosses and Skulls

When we entered the black forest, and passed through the dark pine woods, then the stories of robbers began, just as people at sea seem to take a particular pleasure in talking of shipwrecks. Every cross had its tale of murder, and by the way, it seems to me, that a work written with connaissance de cause, and entitled 'History of the Crosses', though it might not equal the 'History of the Crusades', would be quite as interesting, and much more romantic, than the Newgate Calendar. The difficulty would consist in procuring authentic information concerning them. There were a lady and two gentlemen in the diligence, and the lady seemed to be very much au fait as to their purport and history. Under one her own servant was buried, and she gave rather a graphic account of his murder. He was sitting outside, on the top of the diligence. The party within were numerous but unarmed. Suddenly a number of robbers with masks on came shouting down upon them from amongst the pine trees. They first took aim at the poor mozo, and shot him through the heart. He fell, calling in piteous tones to a padre who was in the coach, entreating him to stop and confess him, and groaning out a farewell to his friend the driver. Mortal fear prevailed over charity both in priest and layman, and the coachman, whipping up his horses, passed at full gallop over the body of the murdered man, so that, the robbers being on foot, the remainder of the party escaped.

Whilst we were listening to tales of blood and murder, our escort took leave of us, supposing we should meet another immediately, whereas we found that we had arrived at the most dangerous part of the road, and that no soldiers were in sight. We certainly made up our minds to an attack this time, and got ready our rings and watches, not to hide, but to give, for we womenkind were clearly of opinion, that in case of an attack, it was much better to attempt no defence, our party having only two guns amongst them.

In a woody defile there is a small clear space called Las Cruces, where several wooden crosses point out the site of a famous battle between the curate Hidalgo and the Spanish General Truxillo. An object really in keeping with the wild scenery was the head of the celebrated robber

Maldonado, *nailed to the pine-tree beneath which he committed his last murder. It is now quite black, and grins there, a warning to his comrades and an encouragement to travelers. From the age of ten to that of fifty, he followed the honourable profession of free-trader, when he expiated his crimes. The padre who was in the coach with us told us that he had heard his last confession. That grinning skull was once the head of a man, and an ugly one too, they say; but stranger still it is to think that that man was once a baby, and sat on his mother's knee, and that his mother may have been pleased to see him cut his first tooth. If she could but see his teeth now! Under this very head, and as if to show their contempt for law and justice, the robbers lately eased some travelers of their luggage. Those who were robbed, however, were false coiners, rather a common class in Toluca, and two of these ingenious gentlemen were in the coach with us (as we afterwards learnt), and were returning to that city. These, with the brandy-drinking female, composed our select little party!*

Frances Calderón de la Barca, Life in Mexico, 1842

An arrest, Agustín Casasola

State of Morelos

The mild climates of the state of Morelos have always attracted more powerful cultures from less agreeable lands. Chalcatzingo lay on the western frontier of the Olmec expansion; a series of bas-reliefs on boulders here give glimpses into the Olmec religion. Xochicalco just southwest of Cuernavaca became an important center just after the fall of Teotihuacán around AD 700. The city was probably inhabited by a tribe of Chontal-speaking Putun Maya from the Gulf coast called the Olmeca-Xicallanca (no relation to the Olmecs); they worshipped the Feathered Serpent that surrounds the main temple here. In 1426, the kingdoms of Morelos were defeated by the Aztecs and masses of tribute were sent over the mountains to Tenochtitlán. The Aztec emperor, Motecuhzoma I, built a luxuriant garden in Oaxtepec near Cuernavaca (then called Cuauhnahuac) which may have inspired the first European botanical gardens. In 1521, Cortés conquered the region, made it part of his *encomienda* and constructed the New World's first sugar refinery. He also built a palace in Cuernavaca to which he retreated whenever colonial politics became too much for him. Many other Spaniards also purchased sugar plantations in Morelos and imported African slaves to replace the Indians who died of disease and overwork. For centuries most of Morelos' land has been concentrated in the hands of a few, usually absentee landlords from Mexico City; agrarian reform has been a burning issue here.

Cuernavaca became the favorite vacation spot of first the *criollo* élite and then Emperor Maximilian; today it contains weekend homes of movie stars and politicians. The first *bandoleros*, peasant revolutionaries, sprang up in 1856 and were later crushed by Porfirio Díaz. *Bandolerismo* returned with a vengeance under the leadership of Emiliano Zapata. After his 'Liberating Army of the South' ousted Díaz's followers during the 1910–20 Revolution, he instituted his own brand of peasant communism and redistributed millions of acres of land to *campesinos*. The rich fled Cuernavaca for Mexico City. Zapata was assassinated on 10 April 1919 in a treacherous ambush ordered by President Carranza. At the end of the Revolution, Morelos' economy lay in ruins and reconstruction took decades.

CUERNAVACA

Morelos' capital, the resort city of Cuernavaca (pop 400,000), lies on the southern slopes of the mountains that ring the Valley of Mexico. The city is famous for its mild climate. At 1,542 meters (5,072 feet), it is substantially lower than Mexico City. It is never too hot or too cold, and even the rainiest summer days are guaranteed a few hours of sun. Cuernavaca has been a retreat of Mexico City's wealthy and powerful since Aztec times. Unfortunately, this garden spot has grown rapidly over the last two decades, leading to pollution and congestion. However, there are still enough trees,

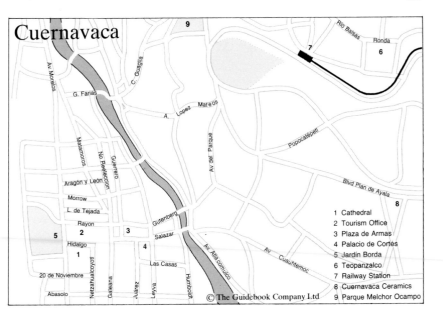

Cuernavaca

1 Cathedral
2 Tourism Office
3 Plaza de Armas
4 Palacio de Cortés
5 Jardín Borda
6 Teopanzalco
7 Railway Station
8 Cuernavaca Ceramics
9 Parque Melchor Ocampo

© The Guidebook Company Ltd

gardens and fine colonial buildings to make you forget urban woes. Cuernavaca remains the favorite weekend retreat of Mexico City's élite; politicians, businessmen, artists and movie stars relax in elaborate mansions hidden behind tall stone walls. The fanciest suburbs, where former President Salinas de Gortari and Cantinflas have homes, are south of downtown.

Cuernavaca is built on a slope, and the city's main street, **Avenida Morelos**, is the old Mexico City–Acapulco road (the new highway bypasses the town). The **Cathedral**, also called the Monastery and Temple of San Francisco, at Avs Morelos and Hidalgo, was begun in 1529 by Franciscans and is the fifth oldest church in Mexico. This building doubled as a fort wherein the town's Spanish population could gather if attacked; the exterior's thick walls, tiny windows and lack of adornment reveal this intention. Just to the right of the entrance is the old **open chapel** where the crowds of Indian converts congregated for prayer. The huge single-vaulted interior was renovated in 1961 with stark ecclesiastical décor and ugly stained glass. During the renovation, they discovered large oriental-style murals on the walls depicting a mass crucifixion. They were apparently painted during the 17th century by a Japanese convert who was inspired by the mass martyrization of 24 missionaries in Japan. One of these became the first Mexican saint. The Sunday masses (11 am) are accompanied by *Mariachis* and are very popular. The **Capilla de la Reconciliación** to the right of the open chapel contains deteriorating statues of saints, a flaking churrigueresque retable and an interesting painting of the Crucifixion depicting soldiers playing dice

at the foot of the Cross. One of Cuernavaca's **artisan markets** stands just across Av Hidalgo from the Cathedral. A few steps uphill on Av Morelos is the entrance to the **Jardín Borda** (small admission fee), once Emperor Maximilian and Empress Carlota's favorite promenade in Cuernavaca. The now-overgrown gardens were laid out in 1783 by José de la Borda, the Taxco silver magnate, and contain paths among many trees, fountains and even a large pool for small rowboats.

From the Cathedral, Av Hidalgo heads east three blocks to the **Palacio de Cortés**. This crenelated fortress constructed between 1522 and 1532 was Cortés' home and from it he controlled the vast holdings he owned as Marquis of the Valley of Oaxaca. A pyramid originally stood at this site, and you can still see some Aztec carved stones in front of the entrance. The palace is now the **Museo Regional Cuauhnahuac** (Tues–Sun, 10 am–5 pm)— Cuauhnahuac is Cuernavaca's Indian name. The first floor contains mammoth bones from near Texcoco and artefacts from sites in Morelos, with sketchy labelling. An exhibition displays the many mutations of the building from a simple fort to the palace you see today. The second floor is devoted to Mexican history from the Con-

Toltec warrior-column, Tula

quest to the Revolution. The highlight are murals along the balcony painted by Diego Rivera in the 1920s under commission from Dwight Morrow, the American ambassador. From the right, they depict Mexican history from Cortés to Zapata in violently anti-Spanish and pro-Indian terms. Here are the battles of the Conquest, the chopping down of the Tree of Life, enslavement, evangelization by evil priests, plantation labor, the Inquisition and, finally, the peasant revolutionary, Emiliano Zapata, to the rescue. A cartoon-like, two-tone mural below the main scenes echoes these topics. There are also portraits of Zapata and the Insurgent general, José María Morelos, who was held captive in this building. A huge black stone statue of Morelos stands in a little square just south of the palace. The plaza just across from the palace entrance is usually filled with artisans making and selling crafts.

The tree-filled **Plaza de Armas** next door, Cuernavaca's main square, is surrounded by pleasant, pricey outdoor cafés, with many insistent crafts vendors. A few blocks east of the train station (a long walk to the northeast, try a cab) is the small Aztec site of **Teopanzolco**. Some of these buildings may actually have been under construction at the time of the Conquest. The structures are built around a grassy plaza, and the largest is the **Temple of Tláloc-Huitzilopochtli**. This twin-staircased pyramid may have been a smaller replica of the Great Temple in Mexico City, because it was dedicated to the same gods. At the top of the stairs, there is a moat-like gap exposing the earlier pyramid on which the larger one was superimposed. Behind this structure is a smaller temple called the **Temple of Tezcatlipoca** ('Smoking Mirror'). Cuernavaca's most famous hotel is the very expensive **Las Mañanitas** at Av Morelos and Calle Linares; it is worth a visit to see the beautiful colonial building and the grounds filled with strolling peacocks and other exotic birds. The **Arena Isabel** for weekly professional wrestling and boxing matches is on Blvd Juárez a block south of the Palacio de Cortés. Pullman de Morelos, with a terminal at Av del Parque just west of the train station, is the main bus line for Mexico City. The Flecha Roja bus line, which runs the Acapulco–Mexico City route, has its terminal at Av Morelos between calles Arista and Victoria. The local university and many private schools offer popular Spanish language courses.

TEPOZTLÁN

A road due east from the north end of Cuernavaca runs 26 kilometers (16 miles) to Tepoztlán at the base of the wildly scenic Cerro de Tepozteco. In the 1960s the town gained a reputation as a hippie haven; vegetarian restaurants and eastern crafts and tie-dye stores are still found around the main plaza. Recently, Tepoztlán has attracted weekenders from Mexico City, some of whom have constructed fancy second (or third) homes in the surrounding fields. The main plaza is notable for its fort-like **Dominican convent** (begun 1565). The church is relatively elaborate, with a plater-

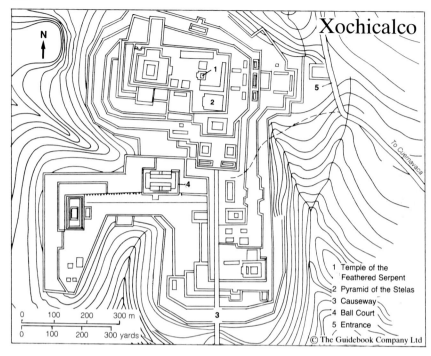

Xochicalco

1 Temple of the
  Feathered Serpent
2 Pyramid of the Stelas
3 Causeway
4 Ball Court
5 Entrance

0   100   200   300 m
0   100   200   300 yards

© The Guidebook Company Ltd

esque portal and *trompe l'oeil* frescoes around the altar. The monastery, containing frescoed cloisters and an open chapel, is more austere. The town's pre-Lenten **carnival** is famous for its masked dancers. A cobblestone street from the plaza leads up to the hillside, somewhere on top of which lies the **Tepoztlán ruins**. To reach them, you must climb a steep rocky staircase and a three-meter (ten-foot) ladder (not recommended for those with a fear of heights). The climb takes at least 40 minutes and should not be attempted by those in poor physical condition. The ruins are open 9 am–4.30 pm; if you arrive on top at 4.31, it is too late. They are closed, no matter how far you have climbed. On top is a soda vendor, a spectacular view and one small **pyramid** (dated 1502). The latter, 20 meters (66 feet) tall, is extremely well preserved; steep steps lead up to a sanctuary with carved columns on top. More foundations and artificial terraces are visible along the surrounding hillside. A huge statue of Tepoztecatl, a legendary warrior, was also found on the site.

XOCHICALCO

The ruins of Xochicalco are reached by turning right off Mexico 95 at a point 25 kilometers (15.5 miles) south of Cuernavaca and taking the *ruinas* road a few kilometers west. The site is five kilometers (three miles) further on the top of a hill. Founded around AD 650, Xochicalco was probably inhabited by the Olmeca-Xicallanca, a tribe of Putun Maya from the Gulf coast. They surrounded the hilltop with fortifications and built stone causeways to outlying settlements. Their rule lasted until about AD 900, when the city was mysteriously burned and the temples destroyed. A path leads from the parking center up the northeast face of the hill. Here is a ball court undergoing excavation. The hillside is perforated with caves and tunnels. One of these was probably used as an observatory, because it has a skyshaft through which the sun's rays reached the cave floor only on the summer solstice. At the summit of the hill stands the **Temple of the Feathered Serpent**, which is built on a patio whose other three structures are still in ruins. The temple is a tall platform surrounded by a deep relief of the feathered serpent undulating around figures of seated, elaborately dressed men. This sculpture is in remarkably good condition; remains of red pigment may still be seen in the crevices. On the top of the platform, the outside of the sanctuary wall is decorated with another frieze.

You will find more ruins down the hillside to the southwest. Here is the **Pyramid of the Stelas** (no stelas in sight); below, another ruined temple slopes down to a patio with two temple-platforms and a deteriorating stela in the middle. Down the hill is a second ball court and remains of another temple. More foundations cover the surrounding hillsides; in fact, only a fraction of the site has been excavated. At its height, Xochicalco must have been impressive indeed.

The rarely visited site of **Chalcatzingo** lies south of the Cuautla–Izúcar de Matamoros road, near the town of Jonacatepec (almost at the Puebla border). The ruins are situated at the base of three 300-meter (986-foot) tall rocks that rise dramatically out of the arid valley floor. The base of the rockfaces and large boulders scattered nearby are carved with Olmec-style reliefs depicting rulers, warriors and deities. The actual settlement can be seen in platform mounds and terraces at the foot of the rocks.

TAXCO

Situated in the dry hills of northern Guerrero, the colonial silver mining city of Taxco (pop 120,000)—pronounced and spelled 'Tasco' by locals—has been attracting tourists for centuries. The authorities aim to keep it that way; development is

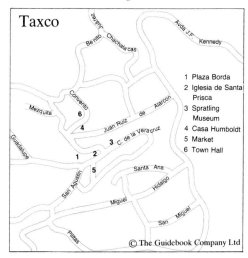

restricted and all new construction, including the gas stations, must have white-washed walls and red tile roofs. Although the silver mines are depleted (nearby fluorite and mercury mines are still producing), the city is now a center for silver jewelry manufacture and attracts buyers from around the world. The road from Mexico City passes the arches of an old **aqueduct** and then becomes Avenida John F Kennedy, along which you find the **tourism office** and the **bus stations**. Above this avenue, Taxco's winding streets all end up at the **Plaza Borda**, the main square named after the town's 18th-century benefactor, José de la Borda. According to local legend, Borda discovered the incredibly rich San Ignacio silver lode when his horse stumbled and broke open a rock to display pure silver ore.

As a way of giving thanks for this bounty, Borda built the **Iglesia de Santa Prisca** (1751–59), Taxco's great churrigueresque jewel, right on the plaza. No expense was spared, inside or out. The pink stone façade, which is best viewed at sunset, is an incredibly complicated intertwining mass of decoration and sculpture. It resembles nothing so much as a frozen baroque symphony. The central panel, depicting Christ's Assumption, floats above the papal symbol of St Peter's keys and hat. The façade is only a warm-up for the interior, which contains nine gilt churrigeresque altars whose decoration, teeming with painted saints and cherubim, is even more complicated than the exterior. Under the arched painting of Santa Prisca, a Roman martyr, is the entrance to the **Chapel of the Indians**, with three more gilt altars. The **Sacristy** contains masterpieces by Miguel Cabrera (1695–1768), a Zapotec Indian painter, depicting the life of the Virgin Mary. The church's jewel-encrusted monstrance (the receptacle for the Host in mass), the most expensive religious object ever made in the New World, currently resides in Notre Dame in Paris. During Holy Week before Easter, the Society of Penitents, a local Catholic association, performs a 'solemn and interesting' procession: the arms of black-hooded *encruzados* are bound to 100-pound bundles of thorny branches; the *animas*, who represent souls in Purgatory, are chained together; and *Los Cristos* carry crosses and pause now and then to flagellate themselves with leather straps lined with tacks. Borda went broke when San Ignacio dried up and, after a string of failures, found an even bigger silver lode in Zacatecas.

The **Museo Guillermo Spratling** on Calle Veracruz behind the church contains the archeological collection of William Spratling, the American architecture professor who came to Taxco in 1930 and opened the first silver workshop here. Spratling taught many local craftsmen and is responsible for the jewelry boom that continues today. Unfortunately, the museum is expensive, considering the exhibitions, and its collection of Olmec, Maya and West Mexican artefacts is haphazard and contains many fakes (some helpfully marked *reproducciones*). The Taxco history exhibition in the basement is being renovated.

Taxco's Iglesia de Santa Prisca

The **Casa Humboldt**, a block down Calle Juan Ruiz de Alarcón, was the house of the famed German explorer Alexander von Humboldt and is now the state crafts store. Steps at the south end of the plaza lead

The ornate façade of Taxco's Iglesia de Santa Prisca

down into the confusing, colorful **market** that fills a ravine between Calles Veracruz and San Nicolás. Here you can find many jewelry wholesalers, retail crafts sellers and vendors of more mundane articles like fruits and clothing. For retail jewelry, try shops around the plaza or the fancy Ballesteros store at 4 Calle Celos Muñoz. Stuart Cohen, a boutique owner from Alaska who buys silver in Taxco every year, gives this overview of the industry.

Taxco's restaurants may be found around the plaza and along Calle San Nicolás. Restaurants Santa Fe and Tía Culla (on the second floor) on San Nicolás are recommended. The cheaper hotels are in the old part of town; the more luxurious resorts lie just off of Av Kennedy on the north and south sides of town.

State of Puebla

The state of Puebla is the site of one of the most important archeological finds in the New World. In caves in the Tehuacán Valley archeologists found tiny ears of domesticated corn dated around 3000 BC. These are the earliest discovered signs of a crop that became Mexico's 'staff of life'; without corn the great developments of pre-Hispanic civilizations would have been impossible. Researchers theorize that corn was first domesticated between 7000 and 5000 BC somewhere in the Puebla–Oaxaca region. The Puebla-area cultures were first influenced by the Olmecs, and then by Teotihuacán and the Totonacs (from the El Tajín region of Veracruz). The city of

Cholula, which has an Olmec-style patio, possesses pure Teotihuacán-style murals on the exterior of the earliest pyramid. Around AD 900 the Olmeca-Xicallanca conquered Cholula and dedicated the Great Pyramid to the Feathered Serpent. By the time of the last reconstruction, this structure was the largest man-made object in the New World and rivalled the Pyramid of Cheops. The Olmeca-Xicallanca were toppled by the Tolteca-Chichimeca in 1292, and by the next century Cholula was an independent city-state. The Great Pyramid was abandoned in favor of a new temple to Quetzalcoatl.

In the 15th century, after decades of war, the Aztecs finally defeated the Cholulans and forced them to pay tribute to Tenochtitlán. By this time Cholula was one of the most important religious centers in central Mexico—they had a temple for every day of the year—and it was also known for the high-quality ceramics that Motecuhzoma II dined off in the imperial palace. When Cortés advanced upon the Valley of Mexico in 1519, he stopped in Cholula, and his subsequent actions in the city are still debated today. The only certainty is that his troops massacred as many as 6,000 unarmed Cholulans in the main plaza. The question is: did he massacre them in self-defense because they were planning to slaughter the Spaniards, or was this merely a way of broadcasting his power and ruthlessness to the Aztecs? Was he just a mass-murderer or simply a clever general? The reality probably lies in between.

After the Conquest, the Spanish destroyed Cholula's 365 temples and declared they would replace every one of them with a Christian chapel (they only completed 40). In 1531, the city of Puebla was founded a few kilometers east, perhaps as a Catholic response to Cholula. With its early ceramic and textile industries, Puebla quickly grew into Mexico's second most important city. Since many religious orders and a Jesuit college were based here, the city also became known as one of the most pious and conservative in Mexico, a reputation it retains today. The majority of the local Indians died in epidemics and their lands were taken over for large farms and cattle estates.

Pedro Infante Lives!

He has been sighted in Argentina and Brazil. Despite his age, his features are as smooth and amiable, and his smile as undimmed, as when he was idol of the multitudes. He hides out to avoid the shame and the prison sentence resulting from his conviction for adultery. Why could not María Luisa grant him a divorce? Or he was horribly disfigured in the plane crash. He sits alone in his room, waiting for death to finally overtake him, his once-glorious voice destroyed by the burns. He cannot bear for his fans and loved ones—all those women!—to see him in this state.

The mythology of Pedro Infante has mushroomed in the three decades since his tragic death in 1957. During the 1940s and 1950s, this handsome singer and actor was El Rey del Taquilla ('The King of the Box Office') and the top radio and recording star. In his life and character he exemplified the best aspirations of the ordinary Mexican. Born poor in the provinces, he was a hard worker who moved to the capital and made it big. Despite his wealth, he was a devoted son and Catholic, a loving father and a warm and *simpático* friend, who never forgot his roots. He rose to fame through his versatile voice, which could drip with so much feeling that it caused both men and women to break down and cry. And, most importantly for the legend, during his life he was dogged by scandal and tragedy.

Pedro Infante was born into a poor family in the Pacific state of Sinaloa. At the age of 12, he was apprenticed to a carpenter and built his own guitar in his spare time because he could not afford to buy one. He moved to Culiacán, the state capital, in his late teens and worked as a barber, singing to the customers in between haircuts. There he met María Luisa León, a year or two older than Pedro, who saw in this youth the raw materials that could be shaped into a star. After their marriage, she convinced him to move to Mexico City, the metropolis, so he could break into show business. Radio was king during the 1930s and 1940s, and María Luisa pushed the painfully shy young man from the provinces to haunt the studios of XEB, the most important radio station after the now legendary XEW. After months of eating one meal a day and haunting the pawn shop, Pedro finally got his break; for six pesos per week he was hired to sing boleros, the romantic song of the moment, on the afternoon show. A nightclub engagement followed, and the manager decided that Pedro should discard the tuxedo and wear the *charro* outfit of a traditional Jalisco cowboy (now worn by all *Mariachi* musicians). This led to a bit part in a *ranchera* film, the Mexican equivalent of the western. Pedro Infante, with occasional proddings from María Luisa, was on his way.

Pedro's film and singing careers developed at the same time. During the 1940s, he became known as the foremost interpreter of bolero *ranchero* songs, a genre that melded the Spanish-born bolero with the Mexican *Mariachi* orchestra. Among his now-classic hits are 'Amorcito Corazon', 'El Durazno', 'Angelitos Negros' and 'Dulce Patria'. His film roles alternated between singing cowboys and poor but honest young men struggling to survive in Mexico City slums. It was as the latter character that Pedro hit the apogee of his career. In the 1948 melodrama, *Nosotros los Pobres* ('We, the Poor'), he played Pepe 'El Toro', a young carpenter with a paralytic mother who is arrested not once but twice for a crime he did not commit. The director was heavily influenced by the Italian neo-realist films, but *Nosotros los Pobres* parts company with that genre by having an abundance of plot twists, breakneck cartoon pacing and a happy ending. The Mexican movie going public did not mind; they saw themselves reflected in the screen, and the movie became the hit of the decade. Pedro Infante and his character became enshrined as the ideal representation of the provincial poor who were flooding the big city's slums and trying to survive in the face of incredible hardships. The movie played for so long—for nearly two decades it played in at least one movie theater somewhere in Mexico—and audiences had seen it so many times that they said the lines along with the characters. It was like an early version of *The Rocky Horror Picture Show*.

With success came money, women and the ability to indulge his hobbies. It is not known how many illegitimate offspring Pedro Infante fathered, although he once confided to a friend that he was supporting 20 children through school. María Luisa found herself in the proverbially awkward position of the spouse who guided her partner to stardom and now found that she had been left behind. Unable to have children, she adopted a daughter, but this did not stop Pedro's wandering eye. Between projects he discovered a new love, aviation, and this became his passion. He earned his license, bought his own plane and became a major investor

continues

in TAMSA, a Mexican airline. Pedro was not the luckiest of flyers; his license was suspended twice, and the passenger in his first major accident was a beautiful young dancer named Lupe Torrentera to whom he was showing off his flying abilities. The press got wind of the liaison and so did María Luisa. Pedro and María Luisa separated, but she rejected all talk of divorce and threatened legal action if he tried to live with anyone else.

Meanwhile, Pedro's film career went from hit to hit. He starred in sequels to *Nosotros los Pobres*, elevated the prestige of Mexico City's corrupt motorcycle cops with *A Todo Maquina* (roughly 'Calling All Cars') and won an Ariel, Mexico's Oscar, for *La Vida No Vale Nada* ('Life's Not Worth Anything'). In his private life the tempest continued. Lupe and he drifted apart after a couple of children, and Pedro fell in love with a young actress named Irma Dorantes who had minor roles in some of his films. While María Luisa was ensconced in Mexico City, Pedro built a love nest for himself and Irma just off the Mexico City–Toluca highway. Named Ciudad Infante, the complex included a movie theater, a barber shop where Pedro could practice his trade, a flight simulator, gym and chapel, all largely built with Pedro's own hands. The attendant publicity incensed María Luisa, the sole 'legitimate' spouse. When she learned that Irma and Pedro had secretly been married in a civil ceremony, she initiated legal action accusing the pair of adultery, the penalty for which was a prison term. The case wound its way through the tortuous Mexican justice system and finally, in late March 1957, a judge ruled in favor of María Luisa. There was a frenzy of speculation: what would the lovebirds do? In mid-April, Irma called Pedro, who was filming a movie in Merida, Yucatán, and told him he must return home at once and straighten this mess out. Early on the morning of 15 April 1957, Pedro Infante took the controls of a TAMSA cargo plane to fly back to Mexico City. Shortly after take-off, the plane crashed and exploded into a fireball in a suburb of Merida. The reason why remains a mystery, but speculation centers on a poorly-balanced cargo load. The occupants were horribly burned and only identified by their jewelry. Within an hour extra editions were on the streets: 'Pedro Infante Dead!' The city wept; two teenagers committed suicide.

Pedro Infante's funeral was marked with great ceremony. The film industry suspended work for three days. The idol's guard of honor at his wake included dozens of celebrities, including Cantinflas, the other cinematic legend of the moment. Motorcycle cops escorted the funeral. At the graveside in the Panteón Jardín were all the most important women in his life—his mother, María Luisa, Lupe and Irma—along with thousands of fans.

Every year since Pedro Infante's death has been marked by solemn rites at his grave. Statues of the idol have been erected in Plaza Garibaldi and in his hometown of Guamuchil, Sonora. His son, Pedro Infante Jr, has tried to prove that he is his father's heir, but, like Frank Sinatra Jr, he does not have the charisma or the voice. The fans pass the time by endlessly debating which of his women was responsible for Pedro's death—María Luisa, because she insisted on charging him with adultery, or Irma for calling him home that day in April. Meanwhile, the legend lives on through articles, endlessly reproduced photos, that golden voice singing 'Amorcito Corazon' just one more time and, most of all, through repeats of his movies week after week on Mexican television.

The Rivals, *a re-enactment*

In 1811, Morelos entered the state with his insurgent army and fought the Royalists successfully for five years until the tide of battle turned. The Conservatives, with much assistance from the pious citizenry, captured Puebla from the anti-clerical Liberals in 1856. On 5 May 1862, Puebla was the scene of the most famous victory of the Mexican army. In a bloody, day-long battle, a troop of 2,000 Mexicans repelled 6,000 French soldiers weakened by Montezuma's Revenge. The hero of the day was a young general named Porfirio Díaz, who catapulted to fame and eventually became Mexico's supreme dictator. The French returned a year later and bombarded and besieged Puebla. After two months of starvation and shell-shock, the Mexicans surrendered the city.

In 1910, a revolutionary activist named Aquiles Serdán was on the verge of calling for the armed overthrow of the dictator Díaz when soldiers encircled his house in downtown Puebla and massacred him and his family, making them the first martyrs of the Mexican Revolution. The 1910–20 economic and political chaos led to severe starvation in Puebla and other cities. In 1920, President Carranza, on the run from Alvaro Obregón's army, was assassinated in the small town of Tlaxcalantongo by an Obregonista in his own bodyguard. Two of Puebla's post-Revolution governors, Manuel Avila Camacho and Gustavo Díaz Ordaz (a dour conservative responsible for the 1968 Tlatelolco student massacre), have gone on to become president.

PUEBLA

Puebla (pop 1,885,000), the state capital, lies in a broad valley due east of Mexico City. The snow-capped cones of Popocatépetl and Iztaccíhuatl dominate the western horizon, while a third volcano, La Malinche, stands about 30 kilometers (19 miles) to the northeast. The valley's weather is always a little cooler and wetter than Mexico City. Puebla was Mexico's second largest city until this century when it was eclipsed by Guadalajara and Monterrey. Although Puebla is attempting an industrial comeback—there is a huge Volkswagen plant on the northern outskirts—the city's colonial core remains intact and covered with *azulejos*, the ornate local tiles. Puebla is built on a grid pattern: the main axes, Avdas 16 de Septiembre and 5 de Mayo (same street, different names) divide the town east–west; Avs Reforma and Camacho do the same north–south; all four avenues cross in the Zócalo. The huge, stern-looking **Cathedral** (begun 1539) occupies the south side of the **Zócalo**, a typical Mexican plaza with trees, benches and a fountain. One of the largest church structures in Mexico, the Cathedral possesses twin 69-meter (227-foot) towers, the country's tallest, and a tile-covered dome. A little door in the north tower is open mornings from 11 am to 12 noon and leads up to the bells and a sweeping view over Puebla. The vast interior is decorated with marble floors, onyx and gold leaf. The carved wood choir and the enormous organ overhead are particularly impressive. The main altar is one of Manuel Tolsá's greatest achievements—a miniature temple within the Cathedral with a beautiful tiled dome that is a copy of St Peter's in Rome. Behind the altar is a stone retable with solomonic columns; a huge painting depicting the Ascension

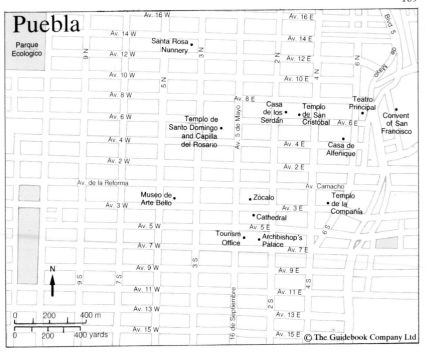

and Coronation of the Virgin Mary covers the wall above. The **tourism office** lies directly behind the Cathedral on Calle 5 Oriente. Next door stands the **Archbishop's Palace**, which houses the **Casa de Cultura** with temporary exhibitions, concerts and movie screenings on the first floor. The second floor is the **Biblioteca Palafoxiana**, a collection of rare books and manuscripts founded in 1647 and named after Puebla's most famous bishop, Juan de Palafox y Mendoza. The admission charge is N$10 is charged (students and certified teachers with I.D. receive a discount), but it costs nothing to stand in the doorway and look at the three stories of carved wooden bookshelves holding thousands of old books that give off a pleasant, musty odor. The **Museo de Arte José Luis Bello y González**, two blocks west of the Cathedral on Calle 3, is an amazing collection of decorative art amassed by a local businessman; it includes tiles, paintings made from feathers, ivory carvings, strange locks and ornate inlaid furniture. Puebla's newest museum is the **Museo Amparo** at the corner of Avs 2 Sur and 9 Ote. Inaugurated in 1991 in an 18th-century hospital building, the museum contains high quality archeological and colonial collections with multi-media displays and labeling in Spanish and English. The first floor is devoted to introductory exhibitions and artefacts from the earliest Mesoamerican cultures of Central Mexico. On the second floor are displays of pieces from the Classic era up to the Conquest. The museum's organization is slightly confusing. The displays are divided first by region and then by function of the objects, and sometimes the distinction becomes blurred. The

Detail of carving by Indian craftsmen

final pre-Columbian room is devoted to sculptural masterworks from the museum's collection. The rooms that follow house the colonial collections of religious painting, sculpture and furniture.

A two block walk north of the Zócalo on 5 de Mayo takes you to the **Templo de Santo Domingo**, a relatively stern baroque church housing the most important and ornate shrine in Puebla. The main church contains a large baroque retable covered with sculptures, two smaller churrigueresque retables and an onyx pulpit. Just to the left of the main altar, the **Capilla del Rosario**, built by the Dominicans in 1534, takes your breath away. Above a dust guard of painted tiles that rises to shoulder level, it is covered all the way to the ceiling's point with gilt carvings. Vine-like tendrils curl everywhere, bursting out of the almost invisible architectural elements with grape and animal motifs. Six paintings of the Virgin's life ring the walls, and grotesque heads at the base or on top of each spew forth the vines that constitute their frames. The dome holds eight sculptures of the Divine Spirits, including Intellect, Fortitude and Piety. Across the entry range the heads of a heavenly choir, and brightly painted—almost cartoonish—saints' sculptures extend from the walls. The centerpiece of the chapel is the altar, a miniature temple made from onyx and gilt solomonic columns that hold up a dome covered with saints' sculptures and the Holy Ghost on top. The altar houses the doll-like figure of the Virgen del Rosario, one of the most venerated images in Mexico. As the patron of seafarers, on holy days she wears a robe made of three kilograms of pearls donated by sailors.

The **Mercado Victoria** one block north was once Puebla's main market but is now mostly closed for renovations. Two blocks northeast, on Calle 3 Norte between Avs 12 and 14, stands the **Santa Rosa Nunnery** (17th century), where Puebla's most famous culinary contribution to the world, *mole poblano* (a thick, dark sauce made from chocolate, chilli and ground spices), was supposedly invented. The nunnery, which is built around two cloisters, has just been renovated and houses the **Casa de Artesanías**; you can purchase unique local crafts in the large store and take a guided tour of the famous kitchen. Another nunnery, **Santa Mónica** (1688) at the corner of Av 18 and 5 de Mayo, is now the **Museo de Arte Religioso**. The building contains hidden passages that were supposedly used to hide nuns during Mexico's long period of clerical persecution. The

The main altar at Santa Maria, Tonantzintla

museum's collection includes many hair shirts, studded thongs for whipping and belts with tacks pointing inward—relics of the nuns' enthusiastic self-mortification. Less macabre religious art and time-consuming crafts produced by the nuns are also on display. Unfortunately the museum pressures you to take guided tours with guides who speak only Spanish (with loose dental plates at that). One block east of the Capilla del Rosario on Calle 2 North and Av 6 East, the **Casa de los Serdán** was the home of Serdán family, liberal activists who founded the Club Luz y Progresso ('Light and Progress Club') opposed to the dictatorship of Porfirio Díaz. On 20 November 1910, Díaz's soldiers surrounded the house and, after a long gun battle, killed Aquiles Serdán, his family and a number of sympathizers; they are considered the first martyrs of the Revolution, and the house is now the **Museo de la Revolución**. The interesting, if morbid, exhibits include a cloth dipped in the martyrs' blood, newspaper photos of the battle and bullet holes in the walls. An urn contains dirt from 32 national shrines, including graves, battle sites and monuments around Mexico. The **Templo de San Cristóbal** next door contains onyx windows and a carved ceiling vault reminiscent of the Capilla del Rosario but darker. This block of Av 6 East is lined with shops devoted to the sale of *camotes*, delicious rolls of soft candy made from sweet potatoes and flavored with coconut, pineapple and other fruits. Av 6 runs east two blocks into **Barrio del Artista** and the **Mercado Parian**. Once Puebla's artistic neighborhood, this area is now filled with stores selling low-quality souvenirs. The baroque **Teatro Principal** (1761), one of the oldest in Mexico, stands just north of the gift shops.

Continuing east across the wide Blvd 5 de Mayo (not to be confused with the avenue), you come to the **Convent and Church of San Francisco** (begun 1535). The stark interior contains the body of Sebastián de Aparicio, a monk who built the first roads in Mexico and is now the patron of Mexican truck drivers. Paintings depicting his life decorate the walls. A room to one side is filled with amazing artworks made from votaries given in his memory. Icons of the monk for your dashboard are also sold. Heading back to the Zócalo, you arrive at the **Casa de Alfeñique** at the corner of Calle 6 North and Av 4 East, now the **Museo del Estado**. *Alfeñique* means 'spun sugar' and refers to the frothy white decorations on the building's façade. The interior contains exhibitions on pre-Hispanic and colonial history and local crafts. The **Templo de la Compañia** (1767) at Av Camacho and Calle 4 South contains the tomb of the China Poblana, a legendary local figure. Supposedly a Mongol or Chinese princess, she arrived in Puebla, was adopted by a wealthy couple and became known for her Christian piety. Her oriental dress style became the fashion in the city and is still worn in traditional dances.

A hill two kilometers (1.25 miles) north of the Zócalo on Calle 2 North is the site of the famous 5 May 1862 victory against the French. It is now the park-like **Civic Center**, which includes the **forts of Guadalupe and Loreto**, the **Anthropology and History Museum**, the **Natural History Museum** (under a pyramid) and the bullring.

Mexico's only safari park, **Africam**, with 3,000 animals representing 250 species, lies twenty kilometers (twelve miles) south of Puebla. Thrice-weekly professional wrestling matches are staged at the **Arena Puebla** on the corner of Calle 4 South and Av 13 East. For local culinary specialties try the Fonda Santa Clara and Restaurant La Bola Roja. Puebla's hotels are all marked by large signs with a red 'H' on them. The new **bus station** is on the northern outskirts on Av Carmen Serdán.

CHOLULA

The archeological site of Cholula (pop 20,000) lies in the town of the same name ten kilometers (six miles) due west of Puebla on Av Reforma. Many mini-buses run this route. In pre-Hispanic times this was one of the most important spiritual centers in Central Mexico and contained around 400 shrines and 100,000 citizens. In the center of town sprawls the **Franciscan Church and Convent** dedicated to San Gabriel (begun 1529), with a broad churchyard. The main church is baroque, with 16th-century paintings, but the most interesting sight is the neighboring **Capilla Real** covered with 49 little domes. This unique structure, which resembles the mosque in Córdoba, was originally an open chapel, but in 1731 it was covered with the current roof. The enormous and dim interior contains a number of altars lit by hundreds of candles. The **archeological site of Cholula** is built around the large hill topped with a church two blocks to the southeast. This hill is actually the ruins of the **Great Pyramid**, one of the largest structures of the ancient world. A small museum on the north side of the site contains a good diorama of the city as it looked at the Conquest. An entrance in the opposite hillside leads to a passage that offers a view of the four stages of the pyramid's construction. Branching off from this narrow, somewhat claustrophobic tunnel are the secret stairways used by the priests. Archeologists have excavated eight kilometers (five miles) of tunnels in the pyramid.

Cholula was a major regional center from about 400 BC onwards. It reached its first height between 100 BC and AD 600, when it may have been a competitor with Teotihuacan, and the Great Pyramid rivaled the Pyramid of the Sun. When the Olmeca-Xicallanca built a center in nearby Cacaxtla, Cholula declined; only one thousand people lived here in AD 800. After AD 1200, the Tolteca-Chichimeca conquered the area and founded a major city. They expanded the Great Pyramid and erected a new temple dedicated to the Feathered Serpent (destroyed to build the town's Franciscan church). By the time the Spanish arrived, the Great Pyramid was one of the most massive structures in the world, measuring 55 meters (180 feet) in height and 425 meters (1,400 feet) on each side.

Various stairways up the hill to the small blue-and-white **Templo de Nuestra Señora de los Remedios** (1597–1666) on top. On holy days, processions accompanied by bands, fireworks, flags and statues of saints wind up the hill to the church. At the base of the pyramid's south side, excavations partial-ly expose the remains of the main staircase. Club Med has built a Villa Arqueológica hotel just south of the ruins.

Staking It All

The ball courts were anywhere between one hundred, one hundred fifty, and two hundred feet long. In the square corners (which served as ends or goals) a great number of players stood on guard to see that the ball did not penetrate. The main players stood in the center facing the ball, and so did the opponents, since the game was carried out similarly to the way they fought in battle or special contests. In the middle of the walls of this enclosure were fixed two stones facing one another, and each had a hole in the center. Each hole was surrounded by a carved image of the deity of the game. Its face was that of a monkey.

As we shall see under The Calendar, this feast was celebrated once a year, and to clarify the use of these stones it should be noted that one team put the ball through the hole of the stone on one side while the other side was used by the other team. The first to pass its ball through [the hole] won the prize. These stones also served as a division, for between them, on the floor, was a black or green stripe. This was done with a certain herb and no other, which is a sign of pagan belief. The ball always had to be passed across this line to win the game, because if the ball, projected by the backsides or by the knee, went bouncing along the floor and passed the stripe the width of two fingers, no fault was committed; but if it did not pass, it was considered a foul play. The man who sent the ball through the stone ring was surrounded by all. They honored him, sang songs or praise to him, and joined him in dancing. He was given a very special reward of feathers or mantles and breechcloths, something highly prized. But what he most prized was the honor involved: that was his great wealth. For he was honored as a man who had vanquished many and had won a battle.

All those who played this game were stripped except for their usual breechcloths, on top of which they wore coverings of deerskin to defend their thighs, which were continually being scratched on the floor. They wore gloves so as not to injure their hands, which they constantly set down firmly, supporting themselves against the floor. They bet jewels, slaves, precious stones, fine mantles, the trappings of war, and women's finery.

Others staked their mistresses. It must be understood that this took place, as I have described, among the nobility, the lords, captains, braves, and important men. Countless lords and knights attended this game and played it with such pleasure and enjoyment, changing places with one another occasionally, taking their turns so that everyone could take their part in that pleasant sport, to the point that sometimes the sun set upon them while they enjoyed themselves.

Some of these men were taken out dead from that place for the following reason. Tired and without having rested, [they ran] after the ball from end to end, seeing it descending from above, in haste and hurry to reach it first, but the ball on the rebound hit them in the mouth or the stomach or the intestines, so that they fell to the floor instantly. Some died of that blow on the spot because they had been eager to touch the ball before anyone else. Some took a special pride in this game and performed so many feats in it that it was truly amazing. There is one trick especially that I wish to describe. I saw it done many times by skilful Indians. They employed a bounce or curious hit. On seeing the ball come at them, at the moment it was about to touch the floor, they were so quick in turning their knees or buttocks to the ball that they returned it with extraordinary swiftness. With this bouncing back and forth they suffered terrible injuries on their knees or thighs so that the haunches of those who made use of these tricks were frequently so bruised that those spots had to be opened with a small blade, whereupon the blood which had clotted there because of the blows of the ball was squeezed out.

As some may have seen, this ball was as large as a small bowling ball. The material that the ball [was made of] was called ollin, which in our own Castilian tongue I have heard translated as batel, which is the resin of a certain tree. When cooked it becomes stringy. It is very much esteemed and prized by these people, both as a medicine for the ailing and for religious offerings. Jumping and bouncing are its qualities, upward and downward, to and fro. It can exhaust the pursuer running after it before he can catch up with it.

Fray Diego Durán, Book of the Gods and Rites and
The Ancient Calendar, 16th century
trans Fernando Horcasitas and Doris Heyden, 1971

ACATEPEC AND TONANTZINTLA

The towns of Acatepec and Tonantzintla, immediately south of Cholula on the old Atlixco road (Av Miguel Alemán) from the main plaza, contain two amazing folk-baroque churches with décor crafted by Indian artisans. The first of these is Tonantzintla, whose church, the **Iglesia de Santa María Tonantzintla**, was begun in 1607. The décor took another two centuries to complete. The tiled façade is relatively plain, with candy-cane-like solomonic columns on the tower. The interior contains carving that resembles Puebla's Capilla del Rosario but thicker, cruder and more vibrant. A heavenly choir sounds above the entrance, and the walls are covered with brightly painted carved wood from floor to ceiling. The décor is thickest in the dome, where the apex is dropped seemingly to fit in all the sculptural figures, including the Holy Ghost. The altar is baroque, with solomonic columns, and two churrigueresque retables hang along the nave. During Easter Week, the church is filled with flowers, woven straw and resinous pine branches from the slopes of the nearby volcanoes. The rutted dirt road up to the Paso de Cortés between Popocatépetl and Iztaccihuátl begins just after the railroad crossing, halfway between Cholula and Tonantzintla.

Acatepec, a few kilometers further south, contains the slightly more restrained **Templo de San Francisco**. First built in 1788, the church was destroyed in a 1941 fire and reconstructed in 1963. Every inch of the façade, including the solomonic columns and the bell tower, is covered with brightly painted tiles. The interior is painted yellow and gold, but the carving is not quite as plentiful as in Tonantzintla. The décor of the three baroque retables in the apse continues up to the ceiling and a dome filled with carved angel heads. Grotesque heads over the main altar spout grape vines bearing fruit.

HUEJOTZINGO

The town of Huejotzingo lies on the old highway halfway between Cholula and San Martin Texmelucan to the northwest. The main sight is the fortified **Franciscan convent** (1550–70), which is well worth a detour. The stern exterior is almost without ornament, except for crenelations that run along the edge of the roof. Beyond the plateresque portal, the huge, dim, single-naved interior has Gothic ribbing, baroque retables and barely visible remains of old frescoes on the walls. The windows are made from onyx, which lets in a pale glow. The old convent to the right is now a **museum**. The town of Huejotzingo is known for its *sidra*, a mildly alcoholic, fizzy drink made from apples. Its masked carnival dances are also famous.

State of Tlaxcala

The smallest state in Mexico, Tlaxcala has always been densely settled. After the decline of Teotihuacán, a group of Olmeca-Xicallanca from the Gulf invaded Central

Mexico and built a hill-top city called Cacaxtla. Huge, distinctly Maya murals in intense colors were discovered here in 1974. Around AD 1100 the Olmeca-Xicallanca were expelled by a tribe of Tolteca-Chichimecas later called the Tlaxcalans. Although they lived only 120 kilometers (75 miles) from the Aztec capital, the Tlaxcalans were fierce warriors and maintained their independence through constant battles. When Cortés' army entered the region with the Totonacs in 1519, Xicotencatl, the Tlaxcalan chief, saw that the balance of power in Mexico had suddenly shifted. After some initial hostilities, the Tlaxcalans decided to make peace and add their army to the Spanish force. The Tlaxcalans became the Spaniards' strongest allies and after the Conquest accompanied expeditions throughout Mexico. Tlaxcalan wards were built in Spanish settlements as far away as San Cristóbal in Chiapas and Santa Fe in distant New Mexico. However, the might of the Spanish bureaucracy soon whittled down their privileges, and they eventually suffered as much as the other tribes. Tlaxcala was one of the earliest sites of Christian evangelism, and in 1530 the Franciscans began the construction of one of the first New World monasteries there. Although Tlaxcala adjoins the

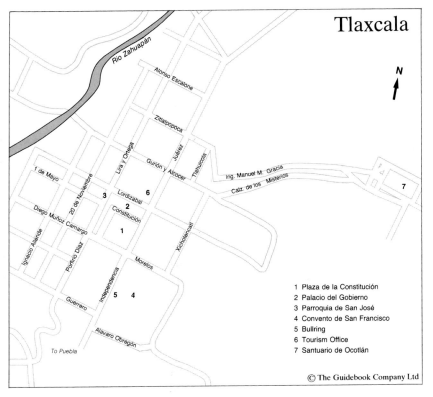

Tlaxcala

N

1 Plaza de la Constitución
2 Palacio del Gobierno
3 Parroquia de San José
4 Convento de San Francisco
5 Bullring
6 Tourism Office
7 Santuario de Ocotlán

© The Guidebook Company Ltd

industrial boomtown of Puebla, the state's economy seems mired in a permanent depression. Vestiges of anger at the Tlaxcalans' collaboration with the conquistadors still may be seen in the way the federal government ignores the state's needs. The only benefit of this situation is that Tlaxcala has avoided the ills of overpopulation and pollution.

Tlaxcala

The state capital, Tlaxcala (pop 36,000), lies along the Río Zahuapán in a valley among scrub-forested hills. It is something of a provincial backwater; however, the lack of development has preserved a traditional pace and some remarkable colonial architecture. The main street is Av Independencia (it becomes Av Juárez to the north) that runs north–south along the side of the **Plaza de la Constitución**, the town's *zócalo* ('main square'). On the north side of the plaza stands the **Palacio del Gobierno** (16th century), with a façade of patterned bricks and ornate windows in the style of Puebla. Originally the Casa Real ('Royal House'), this building was Cortés' home for a while. The interior is decorated with a series of vivid, cartoon-like **murals**, begun in 1965 and still being painted by Desiderio Hernández Xochitiotzin, which depict Tlaxcala's turbulent history. Brightly colored and violent, the murals begin with the first arrival of humans in this area, show the battles and treaties between tribes before the Conquest and so far have reached Independence. A textual legend beneath the paintings interprets the scenes. The Hall of Governors on the second floor contains portraits of all of Tlaxcala's governors. A sweet seed-cake, called *alegría* ('joy'), is a local specialty and sold in the plaza.

The **Parroquia de San José** (18th century) just west of the palace contains some churrigueresque retables and a particularly gory crucifix. To the left of the altar, the **Capilla Expiatoria** is another chapel covered with carvings reminiscent of but not equalling Puebla's Capilla del Rosario. The very ornate baroque altarpiece needs repair. On the west side of the plaza stands the 16th-century **Capilla Real de los Indios**, with Moorish windows; it is now the city hall. The **tourism office** may be found a block north of the plaza on Av Juárez. Steps leading up from the smaller **Plaza Xicotencatl**, just to the southeast of the main plaza, bring you to the entry of the **Convento de San Francisco** (begun 1525). This is an ornate gateway, with a bell tower next door, opening into the cobblestone churchyard. The church/convent complex was one of the first four monasteries in Mexico; the Spaniards baptized four Tlaxcalan chiefs at this spot in 1520 and they became crucial allies of the conquistadors. The exterior of the church is austere and fort-like; to the left is the **open chapel**, where mass was said when the huge crowds of Indian converts couldn't fit into the church. The church interior is lavish; the beautiful *mudéjar* (Arab-style) wooden ceiling painted with gold stars is considered the finest in Mexico. The **Sagrario** on the right contains a three-part baroque altar with vine-covered columns. More baroque retables are found in two smaller chapels. The fountain where the four Tlaxcalan chiefs were baptized is housed in the **Capilla del Tercer Orden**. Next door, the **Ex-Convento de la Asunción** is now the **Museo Regional de Tlaxcala**, with archeological and historical exhibitions, built around a cloister. From the churchyard you have a view over Tlaxcala's **bullring**.

On a hilltop a kilometer east of the city stands the **Santuario de Nuestra Señora de Ocotlán** (1670), one of the most lavish churrigueresque churches in Mexico. You may reach it by local bus or walk east up Calle Zitlalpopoca, three blocks north of the Zócalo. The church stands on the hilltop with a good view of the town in one direction and the Malinche volcano in the opposite. The churchyard wall is topped with points that are repeated along the rim of the church. Except for the façade, the church walls are covered with hexagonal bricks. The façade is painted white and covered with a candy-like confection of elaborate stucco decorations and religious sculptures between the twin towers. The décor actually causes the structure to get wider as it ascends—one of the churrigueresque's most grievous sins in the eyes of the neo-classicists. A huge scallop tops the façade and this motif is repeated inside, but the nave is relatively restrained. Another scallop marks the beginning of the apse, and beyond it the walls are covered with pure carvings. The main altar is one, large tripartite retable that wraps around the walls and rises to the ceiling. Here are myriad saint and cherubim sculptures, and the space between them is filled with gilt vines and rows of flowers running along the structural members. The **Camarín** behind the altar is an octagonal room lined with carvings by Francisco Miguel, an 18th century Indian artist. Paintings on the walls depict the miracle that led to the church's construction: in 1536 a local Indian saw a tree on fire and doused the flames; inside the trunk he found a pine statue of the Virgin, so he proceeded to build a shrine on the hillside for the image's safekeeping. That pine statue is now revered in the church's main altar..

Putún Maya jaguar warrior, Cacaxtla

CACAXTLA

The ruins of Cacaxtla sit on a hilltop southwest of Tlaxcala, just north of the broad plain of Puebla. Look for the enormous metal shed floating up in the hills. Many archeologists believe that the site was a capital of the Olmeca-Xicallanca, a tribe of Putun Maya who flourished in Central Mexico in the 8th and 9th centuries. In 1975, looters discovered a brightly colored mural in the site, and subsequent excavations unearthed another one nearby. They are the best-preserved ancient murals found so far in Mexico. Painted on the walls of Cacaxtla's palaces, they are now protected from the elements by an airplane-hangar-like roof. The murals are sometimes only open in the morning, so it is best to visit then. A **mini-mall** at the site entrance houses a museum, gift shop, cafeteria and tourism office (closed Monday). Those wishing to photograph the murals must pay a fee here. From the entrance it is a one kilometer (0.6 miles) walk by a small pyramid to the murals. The principal structure is an acropolis-like complex aligned north–south on the hilltop. A wooden walkway winds over the building, protecting it from trampling feet. The northeasternmost structure, called the **Palace of the Paintings**, is decorated with a mural on either side of the doorway. To the left, a warrior-knight with jaguar feet holds a stylized lance while standing on a jaguar; opposite, another warrior, with eagle feet and feathers around his shoulders, stands on a Feathered Serpent. The frame around them is decorated with turtles, snakes and snails. The blue-and-red pigment is shockingly intense, as if new.

Cacaxtla's masterpiece is the nearby **Building B** mural facing the north plaza. This shows a gory scene wherein victorious jaguar knights are pitted against eagle warriors. Originally thought to represent a battle, it may actually show the bloody post-battle sacrificial ceremony, with grisly details like a man holding his entrails. Archeologists believe this mural represents a real event that was possibly witnessed by the artist. The **Red Temple**, below the walkway on the west side of the structure, contains more brilliantly colored murals. On the wall of the stairwell, archeologists have uncovered a scene that they think represents the Putun Maya's specialty: trading. A man rests his merchant's backpack on a stick and faces a field of stylized corn, while the scene is bordered by portraits of animals, some mythic, others real (note the remarkably accurate toads). The floor of the Red Temple is painted with grotesque bony torsos representing captives. Further west, the so-called **Star Chamber** contains two pillars decorated with paintings of bizarre blue male and female dancing figures. The male has a scorpion's tail and both are surrounded by five-pointed stars representing Venus (also found in many of the other murals). After seeing these murals, you can almost imagine the psychedelically colored splendor of a major site like Teotihuacán at its height. On the other hand, they bring home how foreign the Mesoamerican cultures were from our own.

Glossary of Language

Spanish is a relatively simple and regular language, and all visitors should pick up at least a few common phrases. Many people in the resort areas speak English, but they always appreciate it when you attempt to communicate in their language. The main difference between Mexican Spanish and the Spanish of Spain is that the former is spoken more slowly and without the Spaniards' lisp. Also, Mexicans have adopted many Indian and American words into their language, such as *tianguis* for 'market' and *el lunch*.

The pronunciation of Mexican Spanish is almost totally regular. The letter 'j' is pronounced like 'h' in 'hat'. In Mexico, 'll' is pronounced like the 'i' in 'machine'. The letter 'x' is normally pronounced like 'h' in 'hat', but may also be pronounced as an 's', 'sh' or 'ks'.

Other letters

a	as in 'father'
b	between vowels, almost like a 'v'
c	before 'a', 'o' and 'u', like a 'k'; all other times like 's'
ch	as in 'church'
e	as in 'set'
g	before 'e' and 'i', like 'h' in 'hat'
h	always silent
i	as in 'machine'
ñ	like 'ny' of 'canyon'
q	like 'k'
rr	rolled
y	like 'i' in 'machine'
z	like 's' in 'sass'

Common expressions

yes	*sí*
no	*no*
good morning	*buenos días*
good afternoon	*buenas tardes*
goodbye	*adiós*
see you later	*Hasta luego*
thank you	*gracias*
please	*por favor*
My name is	*Mi nombre es.../Me llamo*
What is your name?	*¿Cómo se llama?*
How do you do?	*¿Cómo está usted?*
Fine, and you?	*Bien, ¿y usted?*
I don't understand	*No entiendo*
Do you speak English?	*¿Habla usted inglés?*
I don't speak Spanish	*No hablo español*
Pardon me	*Perdóneme*
Excuse me	*Con permiso*
Where is..?	*¿Dónde está..?*
What is..?	*¿Qué es..?*
I want...	*Quiero...*
How much is..?	*¿Cuánto cuesta..?*
Is there..?	*¿Hay..?*
Do you have..?	*¿Tiene..?*
I am lost	*Estoy perdido*
I do not feel well	*No me siento bien*
The check, please	*La cuenta, por favor*
Help!	*¡Socorro!*

Days

Monday	*lunes*
Tuesday	*martes*
Wednesday	*miércoles*
Thursday	*jueves*
Friday	*viernes*
Saturday	*sábado*
Sunday	*domingo*

Time

What time is it?	*¿Qué hora es?*
morning	*mañana*
today	*hoy*
yesterday	*ayer*
tomorrow	*mañana*
week	*semana*
month	*mes*
early	*temprano*
late	*tarde*
later	*después*

Numbers

one	*uno/una*
two	*dos*
three	*tres*
four	*cuatro*
five	*cinco*
six	*seis*
seven	*siete*
eight	*ocho*
nine	*nueve*
ten	*diez*
eleven	*once*
twelve	*doce*
thirteen	*trece*
fourteen	*catorce*
fifteen	*quince*
sixteen	*dieciséis*
seventeen	*diecisiete*
eighteen	*dieciocho*
nineteen	*diecinueve*
twenty	*veinte*
twenty-one	*veintiuno*
thirty	*treinta*
thirty-one	*treinta y uno*
fourty	*cuarenta*
fifty	*cincuenta*
sixty	*sesenta*
seventy	*setenta*
eighty	*ochenta*
ninety	*noventa*
one hundred	*cien*
one hundred and one	*ciento uno*
five hundred	*quinientos*
one thousand	*mil*
one million	*un millón*

Directions

here	*aquí*
there	*allí/allá*
near	*cerca*
far	*lejos*
left	*izquierda*
right	*derecha*
straight	*derecho*
at the corner	*a la esquina*
behind	*detrás*
at the back	*al fondo*
city block	*cuadra*
next	*próximo/próxima*

entry	*entrada*	cup	*taza*
exit	*salida*	plate	*plato*
closed	*cerrado*	bowl	*tazón*
open	*abierto*	bread	*pan*
pull	*jale*	butter	*mantequilla*
push	*empuje*	sugar	*azúcar*
		milk	*leche*
Hotel		cream	*crema*
room	*cuarto*	ice	*hielo*
bed	*cama*	without ice	*sin hielo*
key	*llave*	salt	*sal*
soap	*jabón*	eggs	*huevos*
towel	*toalla*	tea	*té*
purified water	*agua purificada*	beer	*cerveza*
hot	*caliente*	soda	*refresco*
cold	*frío*	coffee	*café*
blanket	*manta*	mineral water	*agua mineral*
pillow	*almohada*	bill	*cuenta*
bill	*cuenta*	change	*cambio*
pool	*piscina*		
credit card	*tarjeta de crédito*	**Locations**	
		bank	*banco*
Restaurant		money exchange	*casa de cambio*
table	*mesa*	airport	*aeropuerto*
waiter	*mesero*	bus station	*central camionera*
waitress	*mesera*	train station	*estación de ferrocar-*
breakfast	*desayuno*		*riles*
lunch	*comida*	ticket office	*taquilla*
dinner	*cena*	post office	*correos*
fork	*tenedor*	ferry terminal	*embarcadero*
knife	*cuchillo*	bathroom	*sanitario, lavabo,*
spoon	*cuchara*		*baño*
napkin	*servilleta*	hospital	*hospital*
glass	*vaso*	gas station	*gasolinera*
wine glass	*copa*	bus stop	*parada*

Hotels

Mexico City and the surrounding states offer a wide selection of hotels, ranging from ultra-modern complexes containing every possible facility to dirt-cheap lodgings for budget travelers. Hotels are regulated by the government's Secretariat of Tourism (SECTUR), and room rates must be posted at the front desk and in every room. Any complaints should be brought to the local SECTUR office. Hotels are inspected twice a year and then rated depending on the type and quality of services offered. The ratings are Gran Turismo (the best), Five- to One-star and Special Category, which is reserved for inns and small hotels in historic buildings. There are also many motels built on the outskirts of Mexican cities; the majority of these cater to guests that do not spend more than an hour or two. You can recognize an hourly motel by the high wall around it, and by the fact that each room has a car port across which guests can draw a curtain to shield their license plates from prying eyes. At a crunch, these hostelries are usually acceptable, except for the constant comings and goings all night long.

PRICE RANGE OF HOTELS IN US DOLLARS
(Mexico City hotels will generally be at the top of these ranges)

Gran Turismo	$150 and up
*****	$60–150
****	$45–60
***	$30–45
**	$20–30
*	Under $20

Mexico City

■ GRAN TURISMO

Camino Real
Mariano Escobedo 700, tel 203-2121, fax 250-6897,
e-mail: mex@caminoreal.com
706 rooms and suites.
Dramatic structure with three restaurants, bars, nightclub, disco, two pools, tennis courts, health club, shopping arcade, next to Chapultepec Park. This is where the élite meet.

Nikko
Campos Elíseos 204, tel 280-1111, 280-9191, e-mail: nikkosal@nikko.com.mx, web site: www.nikkohotels.com,
telex: 176-3523 NIKOME
744 rooms and suites. Four restaurants, bar, disco, health club, tennis courts, pool, business center, executive floors, unusual décor in lobby, on Chapultepec Park.

La Casona
Durango 280, tel 286-3001,
fax 211-0871, 30 exclusive rooms.
Strategic location near Chapultepec Park and Paseo de la Reforma Avenue. A few minutes' walk from the Anthropological Museum.

María Isabel Sheraton
Paseo de la Reforma 325, tel 207-3933, 754 rooms.
Three restaurants, two bars, nightclub,

Charro dancers, Enrique Díaz

pool, tennis courts, health club, shopping arcade, at the Angel de Independencia monument.

■ *****

Presidente Inter-Continental
Campos Elíseos 218, tel 327-7700, fax 327-7730, 659 room and suites.
Well located across from Chapultepec Park, close to museums, shopping and business districts. Executive floors, ladies' floor. Gourmet center with seven resaurants. Extensive conference facilities, well-equipped business center, gym, multi-lingual concierge staff.

Four Seasons Hotel
Paseo de la Reforma 500, tel 230-1818 fax 230-1817,
e-mail: fseasons@df1.telmex.net.mx, web site: www.fshr.com
240 rooms and suites.
Recently built, caters mostly to business travelers. Excellent location near Chapultepec Park and Zona Rosa shopping area. Bars, restaurants, swimming pool.

Crowne Plaza
Paseo de la Reforma 80, tel 282-4244, 625 rooms.
Executive floors, four restaurants, seven bars, nightclub, many top entertainers performing nightly, centrally located halfway between Chapultepec and Alameda Parks.

Continental Plaza Aeropuerto
Puerto Mexico 80, tel 230-0505, 600 rooms.
Two restaurants, three bars, nightclub, shopping arcade, health club, pool, next to airport passenger terminal.

Imperial
Paseo de la Reforma 64, tel 705-4911, 65 rooms.

Converted turn-of-the-century building, two restaurants, bar, convenient central location.

Krystal Zona Rosa
Liverpool 155, tel 228-9928, 335 rooms. Two restaurants, three bars, nightclub, pool, Zona Rosa.

Sevilla Palace
Paseo de la Reforma 105, tel 566-8877, 400 rooms.
Ultra-modern with restaurants, bars, swimming pool, health club, shopping arcade.

■ ****

Calinda Geneve (Quality Inn)
Londres 130, tel 211-0071, 343 rooms. Two restaurants, three bars, Zona Rosa.

Gran Hotel (Howard Johnsons)
16 de Septiembre 82, tel 510-4040, 124 rooms.
Turn-of-the-century building with magnificent art nouveau lobby, two restaurants, bar.

Jardín Amazonas
Rio Amazonas 73, tel 533-5950. Restaurant, bar, pool, near Reforma.

Majestic (Best Western)
Madero 73, tel 521-8600, 85 rooms. 1925 neo-colonial building, rooftop bar and restaurant, cafeteria and magnificent location on Zócalo.

Reforma
Paseo de la Reforma 109, tel 546-9680,

Grand staircase of the Casino Español

200 rooms.
Two restaurants, bar, where the élite met in the 1930s.

■ ***

Cancún
Donato Guerra 24 at Reforma, tel 566-6083.
Bar, restaurant, good location.

Catedral
Donceles 95, tel 521-6183, 116 rooms. Restaurant, bar, recently renovated, just behind the Cathedral.

María Cristina
Lerma 31, tel 566-9688, 146 rooms. Colonial style, restaurant, bar, quiet neighborhood near Reforma.

Marlowe
Independencia 17, tel 521-9540, 104 rooms. Restaurant, parking, near Alameda

Mayaland
Antonio Caso 23, tel 566-6066, 100 rooms. Restaurant, bar, just off Reforma.

Vasco de Quiroga
Londres 15, tel 546-2614, 50 rooms. Colonial style, restaurant/bar, near Zona Rosa.

■ **

Isabel
Isabel la Católica 63, tel 518-1214, 74 rooms.
Restaurant, good location, budget travelers' favorite.

Roble
Uruguay 109, tel 512-3200, 61 rooms. Restaurant, cheap, occasionally dips to one-star category.

■ GUEST HOUSE

Casa González
Río Sena at Río Lerma, tel 514-3302.
Near US Embassy, friendly, meals, call
ahead. No sign—ring the bell on the gate
one door north of Río Lerma.

■ SPECIAL CATEGORY

Hotel de Cortés
Hidalgo 85, tel 585-0322, 27 rooms.
Built in 1780 as a hospital by Augustinian friars, baroque façade, patio fountain,
two restaurants, bar, noisy, on Alameda.

Around Mexico City

TEOTIHUACÁN
■ ****

Villa Arqueológica
Site on ring road, tel 60244, 46 rooms.
Restaurant, bar, pool.

CUERNAVACA
■ GRAN TURISMO

Las Mañanitas
Ricardo Linares 107, tel 14-1466.
Beautiful and famous colonial building,
restaurant, pool and gardens filled with
exotic birds.

■ *****

Racquet Club
Francisco Villa 100, tel 13-6122.
Excellent restaurant, bar, pool, tennis
courts, huge rooms, colonial buildings in
quiet neighborhood north of downtown.

■ ****

Hostería del Sol
Bartolomé de las Casas 107, tel 12-1227.
Restaurant, bar, pool, colonial building.

Posada de Xochiquetzal
Leyva 200, tel 12-0220, 14 rooms and
bungalows.
Restaurant, bar, pool, garden.

■ ***

Papagayo
Motolínia 13, tel 14-1711.
Pool, restaurant, inexpensive motel-style
family resort in center of town.

■ **

Hostería Peñalba
Matamoros 304, tel 12-4166.
Restaurant/bar, garden, colonial.

Roma
Matamoros 405, tel 12-0787.

TEPOZTLÁN
■ ***

Posada del Tepozteco
Av Paraiso, tel 50010.
Restaurant, bar, pool, garden, colonial.

TAXCO
■ *****

Monte Taxco
Tel 21300, 156 rooms.
Restaurant, bar, tennis courts, golf
course, cable car, above town.

■ ****

De La Borda
Cerro de Pedregal 2, tel 20025.

Restaurant, bar, disco, pool, just outside town

Hacienda del Solar
Paraje del Solar, tel 20223.
Restaurant.

■ ***

Agua Escondida
Guillermo Spratling 4, tel 20726.
Restaurant, on main square.

Los Arcos
Juan Ruiz de Alarcón 12, tel 21836.
Restaurant, pool, terrace.

Posada de los Castillo
Juan Ruiz de Alarcón 3, tel 21396, 15 rooms.
Coffee shop.

Santa Prisca
Cena Obscura 1, tel 20080, 38 rooms.

PUEBLA
■ *****

El Mesón del Angel
Hermanos Serdán 807, tel 24-3000.
Distinctive Frank Lloyd Wright-style complex, two restaurants, bar, two pools, health club, northwest of downtown.

■ ***

Colonial
4 Sur 105, tel 46-4612.
Colonial building and furnishings, restaurant, noisy.

Gilfer
2 Oriente 11, tel 46-0611, 92 rooms.
Two restaurants, bar, modern business-man's hotel in heart of downtown.

Palacio San Leonardo
2 Oriente 211, tel 46-0555, 75 rooms.
Restaurant, bar, neo-colonial building.

Royalty
Portal Hidalgo 8, tel 42-0202, 44 rooms.
Restaurant, bar, cafeteria, parking, on main square.

■ **

Gran Hotel San Agustín
3 Poniente 531, tel 32-5089, 74 rooms.
Restaurant, cafeteria, kiddie pool.

Imperial
4 Oriente 212, tel 42-4980, 63 rooms.
Restaurant, parking, downtown.

CHOLULA
■ ****

Villa Arqueológica
2 Poniente 501, tel 47-1966.
French restaurant, bar, pool, tennis, just south of the pyramid.

TLAXCALA
■ ***

Albergue de la Loma
Calle Guerrero 58 at Allende, tel 20424.
Bar, restaurant, near downtown.

Jeroc's
Blvd Revolución 2, tel 21577. Restaurant, bar, disco, pool, north of town.

■ **

Mansión Xicoténcatl
Av Juárez 15, tel 21900.
Restaurant, bar, parking, downtown.

Restaurants

Mexico City

■ MEXICAN

Bar La Ópera
5 de Mayo 10, tel 512-8959.
A popular bar at night, at lunchtime this turns into a dining place for businessmen and *políticos*. Good food, gorgeous carved wood décor.

Café de Tacuba
Tacuba 28, tel 512-8482.
Established 1912, regional specialties, good bakery, colonial atmosphere.

Focolare
Hamburgo 87, tel 511-2679.
Zona Rosa mansion serving gourmet Mexican, with music.

Fonda del Recuerdo
Bahía de las Palmas 39, tel 254-8107.
Veracruz-style, with matching music.

Fonda del Refugio
Liverpool 166, tel 528-5823.
Regional specialties, perhaps the best in the city.

Fonda Santa Anita
Londres 38, tel 514-4720.
Zona Rosa.

Hacienda de los Morales
Vazquez de Mella 525, tel 540-3225.
Colonial estate serving barbecue and regional cuisine, popular weekend family place, south of town.

Hostería de Santo Domingo
Belisario Domínguez 72, tel 510-1434.
Since 1860, Mexico City's oldest restaurant, fine décor, known for its regional cuisine.

La Casa de las Sirenas
Guatemala 32, tel 704-3345.
From a rooftop terrace behind the Cathedral, you can look over colonial downtown and dine on delicious Mexican specialties.

Los Almendros
Campos Eliseos 164, tel 531-7307.
A branch of the famous Yucatecan restaurant chain, this is a good place to try specialties such as *cochinita pibil*.

■ CAFÉS

Café La Blanca
5 de Mayo 40, tel 510-0399.
A favorite for inexpensive breakfast, lunch or dinner.

Sanborn's, Casa de los Azulejos branch
Av Madero 4, tel 512-2233.
Locals line up to get into this restaurant, not so much for the food as the beautiful courtyard setting. Come for breakfast.

■ CONTINENTAL

Bellinghausen
Londres 95, tel 511-1056.
Mexican-style steak and seafood, wood panelling.

Cicero
Londres 195, tel 525-6530.
Mansion, expensive, formal, oyster bar.

Delmonico's
Londres 87, tel 514-7003.
Fancy, expensive, steaks a specialty.

Prendes
16 de Septiembre 10-C, tel 747-0082.
Faded elegance, murals, good seafood.

San Angel Inn
Palmas 50, tel 548-6746.
Famous colonial mansion, resting on
its reputation for elaborate Mexican-
Continental cuisine.

■ FRENCH

Champs Élysées
Amberes 1, tel 514-0450.
Classic cuisine.

Les Moustaches
Río Sena 88, tel 533-3390.
French and international, near US Embassy.

L'Estoril
Genova 75, 511-3421.
Small, popular at lunch.

Normandie
Niza 5, tel 533-0906.

Rivoli
Hamburgo 123, tel 525-6862.

Christmas diorama, the Zócalo

Foundry workers, Agustín Casasola

■ ITALIAN

Alfredo's
Genova 74, tel 511-3864.

La Pergola
Londres 107, tel 511-3049.
Two others around town, good reputation, popular.

■ SPANISH

Casino Español
Isabel la Católica 31, 2nd fl, tel 585-1093.
Traditional, big portions, peek into the Hall of Mirrors next door.

Círculo Vasco Español
16 de Septiembre 57, 1st fl, tel 518-2908.
Colonial building, good seafood.

Mesón del Cid
Humboldt 1, tel 512-7629.
Renowned Catalan cuisine.

■ SEAFOOD

Danubio
Uruguay 3, tel 521-0976.
Spanish style, good lunch specials.

Nuevo Acapulco
López 9, tel 521-1982.
Period 1930s décor.

■ VEGETARIAN

El Vegetariano
Filomeno Mata 13.
Inexpensive.

Yug
Varsovia 3.
Zona Rosa, cheap.

Around Mexico City

■ CUERNAVACA

Baalbek
Netzahualcoyotl 300 at Motolinia.
Expensive Lebanese in Arabian Nights setting.

Las Mañanitas
Ricardo Linares 107.
Posh continental in a stunning garden setting punctuated by strutting exotic birds.

■ TAXCO

Alarcón
Palma 2.
On the plaza,
Mexican and international.

Santa Fe
San Nicolás.
Good Mexican, inexpensive.

Tía Culla
San Nicolás, 2nd fl.
Regional specialties, *pozole*.

■ PUEBLA

Fonda Santa Clara
3 Poniente 307.
Local specialties, *mole*.

La Bola Roja
17 Sur 1305.
Mole, *chalupas*, maguey worms and other regional food.

La Poblanita
10 Norte 1404-B.
Mole and other local food.

Recommended Reading

Archeology and Anthropology

Bierhorst, John, *Cantares Mexicanos (Songs of the Aztecs)* (Stanford University Press, Stanford, 1985)

Clendinnen, Inga, *Aztecs* (Cambridge University Press, Cambridge, 1991)

Coe, Michael, Dean Snow, and Elizabeth Benson, *Atlas of Ancient America* (Facts on File, New York, 1986)

Coe, Michael, *The Maya* (Thames and Hudson, London, 1993)

Coe, Michael, *Mexico* (Thames and Hudson, London, 1994)

Davies, Nigel, *The Aztecs* (Macmillan, London, 1973)

Davies, Nigel, *The Toltec Heritage: from the Fall of Tula to the Rise of Tenochtitlán* (University of Oklahoma Press, Norman, 1980)

Davies, Nigel, *The Toltecs, until the Fall of Tula* (University of Oklahoma Press, Norman, 1987)

Durán, Fray Diego, *Book of the Gods and Rites and The Ancient Calendar* (University of Oaklahoma Press, 1971)

Léon-Portilla, Miguel, *Pre-Columbian Literatures of Mexico* (University of Oklahoma Press, Norman, 1969)

Léon-Portilla, Miguel, *Aztec Thought and Culture* (University of Oklahoma Press, Norman, 1963)

Matos Moctezuma, Eduardo, *The Aztecs* (Rizzoli, New York, 1989)

Miller, Mary Ellen, *The Art of Mesoamerica, from Olmec to Aztec* (Thames and Hudson, London, 1986)

Miller, Mary Ellen and Karl Taube, *The Gods and Symbols of Ancient Mexico and the Maya* (Thames and Hudson, London, 1993)

O'Crouley, Don Pedro Alonso, *A Description of The Kingdom of New Spain, 1774* (John Howell, 1972)

Soustelle, Jacques, *Daily Life of the Aztecs* (George Weidenfeld and Nicolson, London, 1961)

Wolf, Eric, *Sons of the Shaking Earth* (University of Chicago Press, Chicago, 1959)

Art and Culture

Carmichael, Elizabeth and Chloe Sayer, *The Skeleton at the Feast: the Day of the Dead in Mexico* (University of Texas Press, Austin, 1992)

Helm, MacKinley, *Modern Mexican Painters* (Dover Books, New York, 1941)
Mora, Carl J, *Mexican Cinema* (University of California Press, Berkeley, 1982)
Toussaint, Manuel, *Colonial Art in Mexico* (University of Texas Press, Austin, 1967)
Weisman, Elizabeth, *Art and Time in Mexico* (Harper and Row, New York, 1985)

History

Bazant, Jan, *A Concise History of Mexico, from Hidalgo to Cárdenas* (Cambridge
    University Press, Cambridge, 1977)
Cortés, Hernando, *Five Letters, 1519–1526* (W W Norton & Co, New York, 1969)
Díaz de Castillo, Bernal, *The Conquest of New Spain* (Penguin, London, 1963)
Kandell, Jonathan, *La Capital* (Random House, New York, 1988)
Leonard, Irving A, *Baroque Times in Old Mexico* (University of Michigan, Anne
    Arbor, 1959)
Meyer, Michael C and William L Sherman, *The Course of Mexican History* (Oxford
    University Press, New York, 1979)
Quirk, Robert E, *The Mexican Revolution, 1914–1915* (Indiana University Press,
    Bloomington, 1960)
Simpson, Lesley Bird, *Many Mexicos* (University of California Press, Berkeley, 1941)

Literature

Fuentes, Carlos, *Christopher Unborn* (Farrar, Straus and Giroux, New York, 1989)
Fuentes, Carlos, *Where the Air is Clear* (Farrar, Straus and Giroux, New York, 1960)
Jennings, Gary, *Aztec* (Avon Books, New York, 1980)
Kerouac, Jack, *On the Road* (Penguin, New York, 1955)
Lowry, Malcolm, *Under the Volcano* (Jonathan Cape, London, 1984)
Taibo II, Paco Ignacio, *An Easy Thing* (Viking, New York, 1990)
Taibo II, Paco Ignacio, *Some Clouds* (Viking, New York, 1992)

Modern Mexico

Buñuel, Luis, *My Last Sigh* (Knopf, New York, 1983)
Lewis, Oscar, *The Children of Sanchez* (Random House, New York, 1961)
Lewis, Oscar, *Five Families* (Basic Books, New York, 1959)
Oster, Patrick, *The Mexicans* (William Morrow, New York, 1989)

The Angel of Independence (also see page 98) crashes to the ground during the 1957 earthquake

Paz, Octavio, *The Labyrinth of Solitude* (Grove Press, New York, 1961)

Poniatowska, Elena, *Massacre in Mexico* (The Viking Press, New York, 1975)

Riding, Alan, *Distant Neighbors* (Knopf, New York, 1984)

Personal Accounts

Bedford, Sybille, *A Visit to Don Otavio* (Eland Books, London, 1982)

Calderón de la Barca, Frances, *Life in Mexico* (University of California Press, Berkeley, 1982)

Flandrau, Charles M, *Viva Mexico!* (Eland Books, London, 1982)

Marnham, Patrick, *So Far From God* (Penguin, London, 1985)

Index